D0358966

ANTONIO CARLUCCIO'S
SIMPLE COOKING

ANTONIO CARLUCCIO'S
Simple Cooking

PHOTOGRAPHY BY
ALASTAIR HENDY

Quadrille
PUBLISHING

To Patatina and Cotechino

Editorial Director Jane O'Shea
Creative Director Helen Lewis
Project Editor Simon Davis
Designer Claire Peters
Photographer Alastair Hendy
Editor Susan Fleming
Food Stylists Rebecca Hetherston,
Kate Habershon, Katie Rogers
Production Director Vincent Smith
Production Controller Marina Asenjo

First published in 2009 by
Quadrille Publishing Limited
Alhambra House
27-31 Charing Cross Road
London WC2H 0LS
www.quadrille.co.uk

Reprinted in 2009 (twice)
10 9 8 7 6 5 4 3

Text © 2009 Antonio Carluccio
Photography © 2009 Alastair Hendy
Design and layout ©
  2009 Quadrille Publishing Ltd

Cataloguing in Publication Data: a catalogue
record for this book is available from the
British Library.

ISBN 978 184400 734 9

Printed in China

My culinary career began some 50 years ago while I was a student in Vienna. On a very low budget, and cooking for myself and friends, I had to learn very quickly how to stock a basic larder, how to buy fresh food wisely, cheaply, healthily and daily (as needed), and how to cook it simply. All my ideas came from a solid foundation: the years I had spent absorbing food facts, techniques, textures and tastes from my mother. She was a passionate family cook who managed to feed her large family well, creatively and very lovingly through the lean post-war years. Vegetables were cultivated in the garden, breads and pasta were made at home, and I was sent to forage for wild foods (I'm still wild about them, especially mushrooms). Nothing was wasted, and any leftovers were utilised in a dish for another day.

So, having been brought up in this wonderful way, I wasn't a complete novice in my Austrian kitchen. I had experienced at first hand how to put together dishes and meals with the minimum of ingredients for maximum flavour and satisfaction, and I knew that you didn't need a great deal of money to prepare good food for yourself. In Vienna, I spent a lot of time in the splendid *Naschmarkt*, a famous marketplace in the centre, where you could buy anything from fresh meat and fish, to freshly grown and picked vegetables and fruit from the countryside. There I could perfect the art of shopping and buying that I had begun to learn at home in Borgofranco.

It is interesting that once you are on your own, you develop a sense of self-sufficiency, and learn how to balance your working or studying time with good and valuable *free* time. In fact, at the same time as I was working happily, I learned to cook well, and discovered that producing food to share with friends (especially female friends) kept me socially busy and content. Those months in Vienna were very important for me, because they helped formulate the base of my future hobby/profession. Because of them, I am what I am today, a passionate, virtually self-taught cook with lots of experience in home cooking.

Although I have since been in charge of restaurants, front of house and in the kitchen, I have always preferred to 'observe', rather than 'run' (which I think enabled me to develop my skills more effectively). I have been lucky enough, through my career, to have visited thousands of Italian restaurants that have let me put my nose in their kitchens to do just that. Often I have been invited to lunch with the Italian owners, and it has been fascinating for me to discover the variety of regional foods they have offered and to have engaged in discussions about the food of their area compared with others, either from north or south.

All this has taught me to be impartial about Italian cuisine, giving preference to dishes that I particularly like, independent of the region they come from. Collecting so much information about Italian food has made me curious about its deeper cultural and historic origins, and I have written several books on the subject. The underlying theme behind all of them is the primary and most significant bit of knowledge that you will ever need to know about Italian food: that it is always very simple, and always uses the best ingredients possible.

So this book is a coming together of all the 'secrets' I have learned over those 50 years. Many of the recipes are traditional Italian, many are classics with a twist and some are my own inventions, but all are easy to achieve and delicious to eat. In some of them I reveal how you can make the recipe a little more special – by adding an extra flavour or ingredient – and in others I tell you how to utilise any leftovers to make another dish. Throughout, the recipes are punctuated with all sorts of culinary tips that I have picked up along the way.

This is a book for all those who would like to be able to cook real Italian food, and who perhaps are just starting on their own journey of culinary discovery. I firmly believe that cooking, whether for oneself, or for family and friends, is one of the most loving of human skills. I wish you good reading, successful cooking and great eating.

SAVOURING THE FLAVOUR

Often a combination of flavours can define a cuisine. Basil, garlic and olive oil must be the defining flavours of Italy, as cumin and coriander seeds are of Morocco, say, and lemongrass and fresh coriander are of Thailand. But combining flavours is an art, and it must be learned. In Italian cooking, the flavours are basic and few, without too much complication. The cooking is simple: keep the flavours simple too!

SALT

Salt is probably the most used flavour enhancer in all cooking, and is an essential ingredient in almost every kitchen. Italian salt is produced mainly in Trapani, Sicily and parts of Sardinia by the evaporation of sea water. This coarse sea salt is what I use in my cooking.

PEPPER

Peppercorns – black, white and green – are the fruit of a vine grown in India, Pakistan and Indonesia. Black and white peppercorns are used a great deal in Italian cooking: in stocks, to season, in salamis and on hams. The most important thing to remember about pepper is to buy good peppercorns, and to grind them only as needed. Like all spices, pepper loses its heat and essential flavour if ground too far in advance of use.

HERBS

Herbs are much loved in Italian cooking. Basil is the favourite (although it originates from India), and its sweetness contributes to salads, sauces (tomato and pesto) and pizzas. Also important are sage, parsley, thyme, mint, marjoram and oregano. Remember that many of these herbs are quite intense in flavour, so they should be used with care. The simpler the better is my mantra!

SPICES

Spices play a lesser role in Italian cooking than herbs, possibly because they are mostly exotic rather than indigenous. There are exceptions, though. Chillies are a popular spice, in the south in particular, where they grow happily in the sun. They are an essential ingredient of many famous Italian dishes, such as the *arrabbiata* pasta sauce. Capers, the buds of a native plant, are also an important Italian flavouring. The buds are cured in vinegar, brine or salt. I believe the salted are best, but they need to be soaked in some water, and drained well, before use.

OLIVE OIL

Where would the Italians be without their olive oil? I much prefer a dish cooked in olive oil to butter; not only does it taste cleaner, it is healthier as well. The better the oil, the better the dish will taste. Remember, though, that extra virgin olive oil should be saved for dressing salads and for drizzling on top of finished dishes – in general, it is far too good to cook with. Instead cook with an ordinary grade (but still good) olive oil.

VINEGARS

Vinegar is a much-loved flavouring in Italian cooking. I love balsamic vinegars, but you don't need to buy the oldest, strongest and most expensive – a medium grade balsamic can also be good. Use it to brush foods to be grilled, or in vinaigrettes or marinades. Wine vinegars, both red and white, are also used in Italian cooking, often enriched with herbs. Vinegars can also be used to pickle vegetables (artichokes, peppers, asparagus, tomatoes and others) to make tasty additions to the classic Italian *antipasto*.

THE ITALIAN LARDER

If you are in Rome, Florence, Venice or Turin try to follow in the footsteps of a housewife out shopping. Italian housewives go to the local market every day, and you will be watching one of the world's greatest experts at food buying. You will learn that only the best ingredients produce the best food and, because she is so experienced, a look, and maybe a little touch, is all that's needed to gauge the quality.

Italian men do not usually get involved much in cooking, as they don't possess their wives' shopping acuity. I, however, helped out at an early age, as my mother thought we children – and there were six of us – should learn as soon as possible. One of the lessons I learned very quickly was that successful food shopping depends on the knowledge of the buyer. Once I was sent to the village butcher to buy some meat for a stew: I returned with sliced meat in a packet. My mother, furious, sent me back to the shop, and I needed all the charm of a 15-year-old about to be severely punished to convince the butcher to exchange the sliced meat for a piece…

The years I spent in Vienna as a bachelor, where I learned to cook properly, were the most influential, and the 'rules' I learned then have remained with me ever since. As well as the essentials and occasional luxurious extras (see right), I shopped every day for fresh fruit and vegetables, and with a few eggs or potatoes around, I never starved. Potatoes and canned or dried beans were very handy for making *pasta e patate* or *pasta e fagioli* (pasta and potatoes or pasta and beans). Meat was an occasional treat and the use of this and cheese was according to my budget (which at the time was very small indeed). I loved preparing soups and *minestrone* – and still do today – making use of leftovers from previous meals. Remember that food is far too precious to throw away.

The essential Italian larder of today need not be much more sophisticated than my original listing and it's still far better to shop for fresh foods as and when you need them. Always go for the best quality you can source. In your larder keep a little of everything you think you will need for making the dishes you like to cook and eat. To keep your larder functional from day to day, remember to replace what you have just used when you next go shopping, and periodically check that items haven't gone past their sell-by dates.

MY ESSENTIAL ITALIAN LARDER

Salt and black pepper
Sugar
Decent olive oil (ordinary for frying,
extra virgin for raw)
Wine vinegar
Onions
Garlic
Some breadcrumbs
Pancetta (or ordinary bacon)
1 can beans in brine
Chilli (fresh or dried)
A few medium free-range eggs
Some potatoes
1 packet risotto rice
2 packets pasta (*linguine* and *penne*)
1 can peeled chopped tomatoes
Some chicken stock cubes (yes!)

'LUXURIOUS' EXTRAS

Parmesan cheese
Dried porcini (ceps)
Speck (the equivalent of bacon,
but air-dried and smoked)
Truffle oil
Balsamic vinegar
Anchovies in oil
Tuna in oil

TOOLS AND COOKING UTENSILS

Every experienced cook knows that the industry has produced a multitude of tools and gadgets to satisfy any requirements. Sometimes a tool can be so specialised that it can only be used for one particular purpose. I remember once seeing a woman in Umbria preparing black truffles with a little knife that immediately attracted my attention. It was so small and sharp that it enabled her capable hands to peel just a very little skin off the precious tuber, so nothing was wasted. The knife was specially made for her.

When you start to cook good food however, you don't need numerous complicated tools. Instead look at obtaining a few basic, easily available items that will make specific everyday tasks easier.

KNIVES
I have a bread knife I bought in Vienna 50 years ago. It is made of very good-quality steel and can cut 'mountains' of bread. If you are only buying one knife at the beginning, it should be of good quality and medium-sized – large enough to chop parsley and other herbs. A small blade for cleaning vegetables and undertaking various other small jobs

will also come in handy. Bear in mind that the sharper the knives are, the better the cut and the easier the job. A knife sharpener then, is another essential.

CHOPPING BOARD
This is vital, and one of about 25 x 20cm, or even bigger, is useful for everything.

SAUCEPANS AND FRYING PANS
For cooking you need at least three pans. One should be for frying, medium in size, and I

would suggest a Teflon coating is quite practical; this can be used also for sautéing and to make sauces. A good pot for cooking pasta or soups, or for boiling chicken or vegetables, is ideally larger at the base and smaller at the top, with a lid. This enables the water the pasta is cooked in to remain at the same temperature, helping it to cook perfectly. A medium casserole dish, ovenproof and heatproof, is useful for all other operations in the kitchen.

It is important, though, when buying pans, to choose a base suitable for the heat source you use to cook on or with. While a gas stove with gas rings can tolerate most pans, if you have electric rings either with a solid top or coils, or a ceramic hob, you need to make sure that the base of your pans touch every part of the surface of the heat source. Otherwise things will not cook properly, and you are wasting energy.

OTHER INDISPENSABLE GADGETS

For me these would be a colander for draining pasta and boiled items, a grater for vegetables and cheese, and tongs. A spaghetti scoop or spoon, or at least a slotted spoon, is necessary, as of course are a couple of wooden spoons and a ladle. A blender, either electric or hand-held, is good for puréeing all sorts of ingredients. You will also need some medium dishes of either china or metal in which to prepare roast or stuffed pasta and vegetables. If you are feeling very ambitious and are planning on making home-made pasta, then you should buy a bigger wooden board than the one suggested above, as well as a rolling pin, or (if you want to make it a lot) a small 'Imperia' pasta-making machine.

All the above pieces of equipment are, on average, essential parts of a normal cooking household. In time, you may become a specialist in food production, in which case you will need a lot more equipment. I believe, however, that the above is sufficient to show what you can achieve with very little. And, more importantly, that you are capable of producing good food.

Antipasti e Insalate
STARTERS & SALADS

The word *antipasto* does not mean, as so many people think, 'before the pasta', but 'before the entire meal' or *pasto*. I adore antipasti because these wonderful small dishes titillate the appetite (if you are short of it), and their diversity challenges the taste buds with salty and savoury, meaty or fishy, sour or sweet, with vegetables cooked in thousands of ways, or elaborate salads – which have begun to be consumed as *antipasti* in Italy as well. An important element is the mix of the freshly prepared and the preserved, for the Italians are very enthusiastic about preserving food: think of porcini (ceps) in oil, *carciofini sott'olio* (tiny artichokes preserved in vinegar and oil), cured olives and even home-cured salamis.

Pinzimonio

RAW VEGETABLE CRUDITES WITH OIL AND VINEGAR

Sometimes, if you happen to sit in a Tuscan, Piedmontese or Roman *trattoria*, without asking for it you are served a bowl of crudités (called *cazzimperio* in Rome). These are whole or cut raw vegetables, usually the freshest of the season, often – a bit posh this – served on ice, along with a little bowl of virgin olive oil, salt, pepper and balsamic vinegar in which to dip.

PER PERSON (MULTIPLY AS NEEDED)

2 spring onions, carefully cleaned
2 tender celery stalks
2 thin slices fennel bulb
2 tender asparagus spears
1 young carrot, peeled and cut into batons
any other vegetables you might find interesting

DIP
about 2 tbsp olive oil
2 tbsp balsamic vinegar
1 garlic clove (optional), peeled and finely sliced
salt and pepper

To make the dip, place the oil, vinegar and garlic clove, if desired, into a bowl, adding a good pinch each of salt and pepper.

Arrange the vegetable pieces on a plate along with the dip. To serve, dip the vegetables into the oil and vinegar, being careful to stir the bottom and mix the ingredients together.

Serve with some good bread. So simple, but so delicious.

Zucchini e Fagiolini alla Menta

COURGETTES AND GREEN BEANS WITH MINT

This dish is a favourite of mine and can be eaten either as an *antipasto* or as an accompaniment for various dishes. The Italians tend to cook their vegetables more than other people – and certainly don't serve them almost raw as the French would. They need to be at the most *al dente*, or 'to the tooth'. To test, stick the tip of a sharp knife into the vegetable: if it offers resistance, cook a little longer; if there is little resistance, it should be ready. But ultimately it is all a matter of taste…

SERVES 4

200g green (French) beans, trimmed
300g small courgettes, trimmed and quartered lengthways
salt and pepper
3 garlic cloves, peeled and roughly sliced
1 bunch fresh mint leaves
6 tbsp extra virgin olive oil
1 tbsp white wine vinegar or the juice of ½ lemon

In a large pan, cook the beans and courgettes in boiling salted water until *al dente*, probably about 15 minutes. Drain both and when still warm put in a bowl. Add the garlic, mint and oil, season with salt and pepper to taste and mix in the vinegar or lemon juice.

Leave at room temperature, uncovered, for at least half an hour to allow the vegetables absorb the flavours. The longer you leave them to infuse, the darker, softer and more garlicky they will become.

Serve with some good bread.

LEFTOVERS
Any leftover courgettes
or beans will be delicious
spread onto *crostini* (pieces
of toasted bread).

LEFTOVERS
If you have any leftover peppers, try blending them to
make an instant pasta sauce or dip for other *antipasti* dishes
such as *Polpettine di Spinaci* (see page 24).

Peperoni Arrosto

ROASTED PEPPERS

Roasted peppers, skinned and eaten as a salad, is one of my favourite pepper dishes. They are most delicious when prepared over a barbecue, but can also be cooked in the oven. You will find a recipe like this in *trattorias* from the middle of Italy right down to Sicily; it is a very southern dish. These peppers are great as an *antipasto*, but can also be served with roast meats, and even with fish.

SERVES 4

4 firm and fleshy yellow and
   red sweet peppers

DRESSING
2 garlic cloves, peeled and coarsely
   chopped
3 tbsp extra virgin olive oil
1 tbsp coarsely chopped flat-leaf parsley
salt

Roast the peppers on a barbecue, turning them over frequently with tongs, until the skins are blackened and blistered. Depending on the flame, this can take quite a while. Don't be afraid of allowing them to become black; they're better overcooked than too raw – but you don't want them to turn to ash!

Alternatively, roast the peppers in a preheated oven at 200°C/Gas 6 for about 30–45 minutes. However, while this method is a little less labour-intensive, the flavour is not quite so good.

When the peppers are ready, put them in a dish to cool a little. I don't think they need to be put in a plastic bag or covered, despite the advice of many other chefs. When cool enough to handle, rub the skins off with your hands and discard, then slice the peppers in half and remove the stalks, inner membranes and seeds.

Cut the pepper flesh lengthways into narrow strips and place in a dish. Add the dressing ingredients and mix, seasoning with salt to taste. You can eat the dish straightaway, or leave it to become cold – but it is at its best the next day, when the flavours have had time to mingle.

Mozzarella in Carrozza

FRIED MOZZARELLA SANDWICH

This dish has now spread all over Italy, although it is originally from Naples and Campania in general. It is found mostly in bars as a lunch-time snack, and is at its best when freshly made and still crisp.

SERVES 2

about 4 tbsp milk
4 thick slices country bread
2 large slices buffalo mozzarella
plain flour, to dust
salt
3 eggs, beaten
olive oil, for shallow-frying

Pour the milk into a bowl. Dip the slices of bread into the milk for a few seconds, but do not soak them – they don't want to be too wet. Drain, then place a slice of mozzarella on two of the bread slices. Place the other two slices on top of the cheese to make the sandwiches. Dip both sandwiches first into some flour seasoned with salt, then into the beaten eggs and leave for the mixture to be absorbed on both sides.

Pour enough olive oil into a frying pan to cover the base generously and heat gently (see below).

Shallow-fry the sandwiches in the hot olive oil until golden, about 5 minutes per side. Serve immediately.

FRYING TEMPERATURES
You can judge the temperature of an oil, whether shallow- or deep-frying, without using a thermometer. Heat the oil until it is just short of smoking (on a thermometer this would be about 180°C/350°F). Pop in a cube of fresh bread, or a small piece of the mixture to be fried, and if it bubbles fiercely and turns golden brown in 1 minute, the temperature is high enough for successful frying. If the bread browns more quickly, temperature is too high. And do be careful with fat and frying, as they cause far too many accidents in the kitchen.

Croccantini di Cavolfiore e Formaggio

CRISPY CAULIFLOWER AND CHEESE FRITTERS

This dish is excellent served alongside *arancini di riso* (see page 104) and is one that my friends always ask for when they come to visit. The combination is very successful, an Italian form of cauliflower cheese!

SERVES 4–6

800g cauliflower florets
salt and pepper
olive oil, for shallow-frying

BATTER

3 eggs, beaten
2 tbsp plain flour
150g Parmesan, Cheddar or Gruyère
  cheese, freshly grated
1 garlic clove, peeled and puréed
1/2 tsp freshly grated nutmeg

Cook the cauliflower florets in boiling salted water until soft, about 15–20 minutes. (A little tip to avoid the strong cauliflower smell is to add a drop of vinegar to the cooking water.) Drain well and leave to cool.

Using your hands, crumble the cooked and cooled cauliflower into walnut-sized pieces and place in a bowl. In another bowl, mix the egg, flour, cheese, garlic, nutmeg and some salt and pepper. Pour over the cauliflower and mix well – but gently.

Pour enough olive oil into a frying pan to cover the base generously and heat gently, taking care the oil doesn't get *too* hot (see left). Using a tablespoon, put spoonfuls of the mixture into the hot oil, and shallow-fry until golden brown, about 3–4 minutes per side. Drain on kitchen paper and serve warm or cold.

TO MAKE IT MORE SPECIAL
If serving the fritters by themselves, you might consider accompanying them with a little spicy dipping sauce. In a blender, combine 4 tomatoes with a little chilli, 1 tbsp balsamic vinegar and 1 tbsp very finely chopped flat-leaf parsley. If you dare (and at your peril!) you could also add a very finely chopped garlic clove.

Polpettine di Spinaci

SPINACH BALLS

Some 25 years ago I invented the recipe for these little spinach balls for a chapter on finger food in a book published by the *Sunday Times*. Since then I have used them in all sorts of ways, most significantly in a vegetarian pasta dish (see page 72), and layered with pasta in a vegetarian *lasagne* (see page 76). They are very simple to make and very jolly.

MAKES 24 LITTLE BALLS

500g spinach, cleaned and
   tough stalks removed
salt and pepper
2 eggs, beaten
a pinch of freshly grated nutmeg
1 tsp very finely puréed garlic
100g fresh white breadcrumbs
50g Parmesan, freshly grated
olive oil, for shallow-frying

Wash the spinach, put it in a pan of salted boiling water and blanch for 2 minutes or so, then drain. Squeeze out as much water as you can, using your hands or pressing in a sieve, then chop the leaves finely.

Put the spinach in a medium bowl and stir in the beaten eggs, a pinch of salt, some pepper, the nutmeg, garlic, breadcrumbs and Parmesan. Mix well until you achieve a binding consistency. If the mixture is too wet, add an extra tablespoon of breadcrumbs.

Pour enough olive oil into a frying pan to cover the base generously, and heat gently.

Roll the mixture into little balls the size of walnuts. Shallow-fry the spinach balls in the hot olive oil until golden, about 4–5 minutes per side. Drain on kitchen paper and serve either warm or cold.

FRYING TIP
With any mixture to be
shallow- or deep-fried,
fry a little of it first, so
that you can taste it for
flavours and seasoning.
If fine, carry on. If not,
keep tinkering until you
get it right.

Pomodori Secchi al Forno

OVEN-DRIED TOMATOES

The sun-dried tomatoes you buy in shops are often too salty and dry, because all the tomato liquid has been extracted through evaporation in the sun. Much nicer are the so-called 'sun-blush' tomatoes, which are far less dehydrated. Tomatoes like these are easily made at home, and you can start with a small batch like this to see how you cope. Use the oblong plum tomatoes, preferably San Marzano as they have the best flavour.

MAKES ABOUT 250G

500g very ripe plum tomatoes,
   cut in half lengthways
salt
1 tbsp dried oregano
olive oil, as required

Preheat the oven to very low, about 50°C/the very lowest gas possible.

Using a small spoon, remove the seeds from the halved tomatoes and discard. Put the tomatoes on a rack, cut-side down, and leave for about for about 15 minutes to allow some of the water to drain out of them.

Line the tomato halves on a baking tray cut-side up and sprinkle each with a pinch of salt. Put into the preheated oven for at least 2–3 hours until you see them shrinking. You want them to lose most of their water but still remain soft.

Take out of the oven and leave to cool. Sprinkle a little oregano and a few drops of olive oil on to each tomato and place in a jar or bowl. Keep refrigerated and eat within a week of making.

TO KEEP FOR LONGER
If you want your tomatoes to last a bit longer, cover them with oil in a lidded jar and store them in the fridge. But make sure that all the water has evaporated first, and sprinkle over an additional 50g of salt.

Frittelle di Pomodori Secchi

DRIED TOMATO FRITTERS

For this extremely tasty snack you can use the dried tomatoes from the previous recipe or well-soaked and de-salted sun-dried tomatoes. A good way to serve these tomato fritters, with drinks say, would be as part of a platter with cauliflower fritters, spinach balls and a pesto dip (see pages 23, 24 and 68). Just don't forget the paper napkins!

SERVES 4

olive oil, for shallow-frying
16 reconstituted sun-dried or
   oven-dried tomatoes
   (see opposite page)

BATTER
1 egg, beaten
2 tbsp plain flour
½ tsp baking powder
a little milk (optional)
salt and pepper

Beat the egg, flour and baking powder together in a medium-sized bowl, adding a little milk if necessary to obtain a smooth, thick batter. Season with salt and pepper.

Pour enough oil into a frying pan to cover the base generously and heat gently. Using a fork, dip the tomatoes in the batter, making sure they are coated well. Allow any excess batter to drip off. Shallow-fry in the hot olive oil in batches until golden, about 3 minutes on each side.

Drain on kitchen paper and serve either warm or cold.

TO RECONSTITUTE SUN-DRIED TOMATOES
Put your tomatoes in a bowl, and cover with water. Leave to de-salt and rehydrate for about 2 hours. They should plump up to a wrinkly equivalent of the original. Drain well, discarding the water.

Piatto di Salami Misti e Prosciutto

AIR-DRIED MEAT PLATTER

Italians love preserved meat, particularly pork, which comes in all sorts of shapes, sizes and tastes. *Salami*, *prosciutto* and the exceptional dried and cured beef, *bresaola*, are often displayed on platters and accompanied by pickled vegetables like mushrooms, gherkins, onions and olives – which can all be bought in any good supermarket or Italian delicatessen.

PER PERSON (MULTIPLY AS NEEDED)

a few slices each of Felino salami,
   Napoli salami and Calabrian hot sausage
a few slices of Parma ham, *bresaola* (beef)
  or *mortadella*
grissini, *crostini* or unsalted crackers

Display the meats 'artistically' on a platter, and bring through to the guests to help themselves. Usually *grissini* (crisp thin breadsticks), *crostini* (pieces of toasted bread) or unsalted crackers are eaten with the meats. It is important that they are unsalted because the preserved meats contain salt.)

The most significant thing about this dish is that you don't need to cook at home, as everything is available from a good delicatessen.

Pâté di Fegatini di Pollo

CHICKEN LIVER PÂTÉ

This recipe originally comes from Tuscany, but I have varied it a little so that it more closely resembles the much talked-about *pâté de foie gras* of goose or duck.

MAKES ABOUT 600G

500g chicken livers
4 tbsp olive oil
1 tbsp each of finely chopped sage and parsley
1 garlic clove, peeled and puréed
salt and pepper
1 tbsp each of good brandy and sweet sherry
150g unsalted butter

Line a suitably sized terrine dish, or 4–6 individual ramekins, with greaseproof paper or clingfilm.

Using a paring knife, clean the livers by cuting away any green patches and membrane, removing the fibres around the centre of each. Wash and dry well, then roughly chop.

Fry the livers in the oil over a medium heat with the sage, parsley, garlic, and some salt and pepper for about 10 minutes, turning, until still pink in the middle. Remove from the heat and leave to cool.

Blend the mixture in a food processor, adding the brandy and the sherry to the machine while operating, for 3–4 minutes, until you have a rough paste. Return the paste to the pan, add the butter and melt over a low heat until the liver mixture becomes very homogenised, a couple of minutes.

Pour the pâté into the terrine dish or individual ramekins, and smooth on top. Allow to rest and cool in the fridge for a couple of hours, until solid. Eat spread on *crostini* (pieces of toasted bread).

LEFTOVERS
A little pâté added to meaty pasta sauces or to meat or vegetable stuffings gives a wonderful flavour.

Piatto di Pesce Marinato

PLATTER OF MARINATED FISH

For this delicious *antipasto* of home-cured fresh fish you can use slices of filleted salmon, swordfish, tuna, trout, herring, mackerel, sturgeon, anchovies, or even sliced scallops.

PER PERSON (MULTIPLY AS NEEDED)

1 thin slice each of 4 types of very fresh fish fillet (see above)
1 tsp caster sugar
salt and pepper

2 tbsp extra virgin olive oil
1 tbsp fresh lemon juice
2 tbsp finely chopped dill

Make sure that all the bones are removed from the fish. Arrange the various fish slices on a stainless-steel platter, sprinkle with the sugar and season with a little salt and pepper. Pour over the olive oil and lemon juice. Sprinkle over the chopped dill and leave to marinate, uncovered, for at least a few hours before serving.

Piatto di Pesce Affumicato

PLATTER OF SMOKED FISH

This dish is more an idea for the lover of smoked fish rather than a recipe, as none of the ingredients need to be cooked. Just remember that for this to work, you must buy good-quality fish.

To make a display for one (multiply for a number of guests), arrange one slice each of four of the following smoked fish – trout, salmon, eel, sturgeon, tuna or swordfish – on a plate. Serve with 1 tbsp creamed horseradish, half a lemon and plenty of brown bread or *grissini*.

Acciughe in Salsa Verde

ANCHOVIES IN GREEN SAUCE

Italians normally use parsley, basil or rocket as the green base for a *salsa verde*, a sauce that is often made with rather unorthodox ingredients by non-Italian chefs. When you come home and feel a little peckish for something salty, these anchovies on toasted bread are miraculous.

MAKES A 300G BATCH

300g perfect anchovy fillets in oil
  (Italian or Spanish are the best)

SALSA VERDE
about 2 tbsp white wine vinegar
2 large slices country bread, crusts
  removed
1 big bunch flat-leaf parsley, very
  finely chopped, without the stalks

1 small chilli, finely chopped
1 garlic clove, peeled and puréed
10 little cornichons (mini gherkins),
  very finely chopped
15 salted capers, soaked (see page 34),
  drained and very finely chopped
extra virgin olive oil, as required

Drain the anchovies and put a layer of them in the base of a narrow, medium-sized ceramic container.

To make the *salsa verde*, pour the vinegar into a bowl, add the bread and soak for a few minutes. Remove and squeeze dry, then finely chop. Put into another bowl with the parsley, chilli, garlic, cornichons and capers, and mix well, adding enough olive oil to achieve a sauce consistency.

Cover the anchovies with a layer of *salsa verde*, then top with another layer of anchovies. Repeat until all the anchovies are covered with sauce. Add enough olive oil to cover everything, and refrigerate for a day, after which the anchovies are ready to eat. Keep refrigerated for up to a week.

LEFTOVERS
This *salsa verde* can be used in many different ways. When making this recipe, you could make double the quantity of the *salsa verde* and use as a perfect accompaniment for any cold meats, or as a tasty dip for many of the canapé-type dishes in this chapter.

Polpette di Tonno e Patate

POTATO AND TUNA CAKES

This recipe uses freshly boiled and mashed potato, but can also be made using leftover mashed potato. Canned tuna, preferably in olive oil, should always be at the ready in a well-stocked Italian larder.

MAKES 10 LITTLE CAKES

550g potatoes
salt and pepper
250g canned tuna in oil, drained and
  finely chopped
30g salted capers, soaked (see page 34),
  drained and chopped

4 tbsp chopped flat-leaf parsley
3 eggs
about 100g dried breadcrumbs
  (see below)
olive oil, for shallow-frying

Cut the potatoes into walnut-sized pieces and boil in a saucepan in salted water until soft, about 20 minutes. Drain well, then mash and cool.

Put the mashed potato in a bowl. Add the tuna, capers, parsley and some pepper along with 2 of the eggs, and mix well.

Shape the mixture with your hands into cakes 8cm wide and 3cm deep. Beat the third egg in a bowl. Dip the cakes in the egg then coat with the breadcrumbs.

Pour enough olive oil into a frying pan to cover the base generously and heat gently.

Shallow-fry the cakes until golden, about 5 minutes per side. Drain on kitchen paper and serve either warm or cold.

TO MAKE DRIED BREADCRUMBS
To make dried breadcrumbs, first cut the crusts off some leftover bread, and let it dry in a 160°C/Gas 3 oven until crisp and crunchy. Put in a processor and blend to crumbs – or wrap in a tea towel, and beat to crumbs with a mallet or rolling pin.

🍴 TO DE-SALT CAPERS
Salted capers are much
better than vinegared ones
(which never quite lose that
vinegar flavour), but they
have to be de-salted. Soak in
cold water for about 15
minutes, spoon away any
remaining salt and dry well.

Uova Tonnate

TUNA-STUFFED EGGS

I can't count the number of times I have surprised guests with this dish, which may be simple but holds plenty of flavour. If you are in a hurry you can buy a good mayonnaise, but it is much better (and not difficult) to make it yourself. You can do it!

SERVES 4–6

6 large eggs
150g canned tuna in oil, drained and
   finely chopped
12 salted capers, soaked (see left),
   drained and finely chopped
1 gherkin (optional), finely sliced

MAYONNAISE
2 egg yolks
salt and pepper
1 tsp French mustard
100ml olive oil (not extra virgin)
juice of ½ lemon

Put the eggs in a small pan of cold water, bring to the boil and hard-boil for 15 minutes. Drain and leave to cool.

To make the mayonnaise, beat the egg yolks with a pinch of salt and the mustard in a bowl until creamy. Slowly pour in a little of the olive oil, whisking constantly until amalgamated. Keep adding the oil a little at a time, whisking all the while, until the mixture has thickened and all the oil has been used. Now add the lemon juice and mix well. Taste for seasoning and cover until needed.

Peel the eggs and cut in half. Remove the yolks, place in a bowl and, with a fork, reduce to a pulp. Mix this with the tuna, capers (reserving a few to use as garnish) and enough mayonnaise to be able to form balls the size of the original yolks. Place these in the holes of the halved egg whites.

Arrange the eggs in bowls, cover with some more mayonnaise and serve topped with the gherkin slices and reserved caper pieces.

Calamari Fritti

DEEP-FRIED SQUID

These deep-fried squid pieces are very easy to prepare and amusing to eat. They can be served by themselves, as here – which is often called *alla romana* (the Roman way) – or as part of a larger *fritto misto*, a dish of mixed fried fish.

SERVES 4

400g squid bodies and tentacles,
    cleaned (see below)
plenty of olive or groundnut oil,
    for deep-frying
50g semolina flour
50g plain flour
salt and pepper

Wash the squid bodies and tentacles and dry on kitchen paper. Cut the bodies into rings about 1.5cm thick.

Meanwhile, gently heat the oil in a deep frying pan. You will need enough oil to enable the individual pieces of squid to float, at least 5cm deep.

Mix the flours together in a medium bowl, and season with salt and pepper. Toss the squid pieces in the flour, shaking off any surplus.

Put a few pieces of floured squid into the hot oil at a time and deep-fry until golden brown, about 4–5 minutes. Drain well on kitchen paper and serve immediately.

TO CLEAN SQUID
Most squid come ready cleaned these days, especially the small ones, but if your fishmonger hasn't done it, simply pull the tentacles and head from the body of the squid. There will be an eye, viscera and ink sac attached to the head, which you should cut off and discard. Cut the hard little beak from the middle of the tentacles at the top, and pull the quill from the body, discarding both. Wash and dry everything well.

Insalata di Rucola, Pomodoro e Mozzarella

ROCKET, TOMATO AND MOZZARELLA SALAD

I like this combination of tomato and mozzarella without the usual basil, which I prefer to eat just with tomatoes. The rocket, particularly the wild variety, revives the rather bland tomato and mozzarella with its sharp taste.

SERVES 4

100g rocket (preferably wild), cleaned and washed
200g tomatoes, quartered
150g buffalo mozzarella, cut into strips

DRESSING
4 tbsp extra virgin olive oil
1 tbsp white wine vinegar
$\frac{1}{2}$ tsp caster sugar
salt and pepper

To make the dressing, combine the oil, vinegar, sugar, salt and pepper in a small bowl and mix well.

Mix the rocket, tomatoes and mozzarella in a bowl and toss together with the dressing. Serve immediately (as the tomato becomes pulpy if left for too long).

Insalata Verde con Finocchio

GREEN SALAD WITH FENNEL

My favourite salads are the simplest ones, where the ingredients – and not too many of them – complement each other. The combination here of crisp gem lettuce and tender fennel bulb is extremely refreshing.

SERVES 4

4 baby gem lettuces
2 fennel bulbs
4 tbsp extra virgin olive oil
juice of ½ lemon,
   plus the finely grated rind, or, if you prefer,
   3 tbsp balsamic vinegar
salt and pepper

Wash the lettuces and cut in quarters lengthways. Pull the leaves apart, discarding those on the outside if not tender. Put in a bowl. Discard the tougher outer leaves of the fennel, then cut the remaining flesh into very thin slices horizontally. Add to the bowl.

For the dressing, combine the oil, lemon juice and rind (or vinegar), salt and pepper in a bowl and mix well. Pour over the salad, toss and serve.

TO MAKE IT MORE SPECIAL
For an interesting flavour combination, try replacing the gem lettuces with heads of Belgian chicory. The natural bitterness of the chicory leaves will provide a nice contrast to the aniseed flavour of the fennel bulbs.

Insalata di Cicoria Belga con Olio al Tartufo

BELGIAN CHICORY SALAD WITH TRUFFLE OIL

I tend not to use too much truffle oil because it is very intense, preferring to eat the real thing in season, but to counteract the slight bitterness of the chicory, the truffle oil is very good. This salad can be served as a starter, but also makes a wonderful side dish to roast beef or fillet steak.

SERVES 4

4 heads Belgian chicory
30g summer truffle (optional), thinly sliced

DRESSING
2 tbsp extra virgin olive oil
½ tsp truffle oil
2 tbsp balsamic vinegar
salt and pepper

Trim off and discard the root ends of the chicory. Cut the white leaves into small strips and place in a bowl.

For the dressing, combine the olive oil, truffle oil, vinegar, a little salt and plenty of pepper in a small bowl and mix well. Pour into the bowl with the chicory and toss together. Serve topped with the summer truffle slices, if using.

Insalata di Cavolo Verza

SAVOY CABBAGE SALAD

I have long and fond memories of this salad. After the war, when I was in my mid-teens, my schoolmates and I were often very hungry in the afternoon. An impromptu afternoon snack of cabbage 'borrowed' from the local farmer, olive oil, vinegar and bread was easily organised!

SERVES 4

1 Savoy cabbage
4 large slices good country bread
1 garlic clove, peeled

DRESSING
3 tbsp olive oil
1 tbsp white wine vinegar
2 anchovy fillets in oil,
   drained and very finely chopped
salt and pepper

Remove the outer leaves of the cabbage (these can be used as suggested below) until you are left with just the white centre. Slice this very thinly. Place the cabbage in a salad bowl.

Rub the slices of bread with the garlic clove.

For the dressing, combine the oil, vinegar, anchovies, a little salt and a lot of pepper in a small bowl and mix well. Pour into the bowl with the cabbage and toss. Eat with the garlic bread.

LEFTOVERS
You will have quite a few outer leaves of cabbage leftover in this dish. Use them shredded in soups, like *minestrone* (see page 54), or in a quick form of *sauerkraut*. Fry them with a little onion, some vinegar, juniper berries, salt and pepper, for a perfect accompaniment to boiled meats, sausages, chicken or roast pork.

Panzanella

BREAD AND VEGETABLE SALAD

My mother used to make this interesting dish for the sake of economy, but I make it because to me it tastes of summer – and none go by without me making it a few times at least. She used stale bread, which was baked in the oven to make it more absorbent and edible.

SERVES 4

4 large slices country bread,
  crusts removed
4 large ripe tomatoes (about 800g)
the tender centre of 1 head celery,
  plus leaves, coarsely chopped
10 basil leaves, chopped
10 pitted olives, green or black

1 bunch spring onions, chopped
1 yellow pepper, seeded and cut into
  fine strips
1 garlic clove (optional), peeled and
  puréed
6 tbsp extra virgin olive oil
salt and pepper

Preheat the oven to 160°C/Gas 3, and bake the bread for about 20 minutes, until golden. Break the cooked bread into small pieces about the size of a large sugar lump.

Put the tomatoes into a bowl of water that has just come to the boil, and leave for 30 seconds. Pull off the skin, then chop the flesh coarsely, collecting all the juices. (If your tomatoes are not very juicy, you'll need some help with soaking the bread, try adding some tomato juice from a carton or can.)

Mix the tomato pieces and juices together with all the other ingredients, including the bread. Leave to infuse for a few hours, so that the bread can absorb all the flavours and soften. Stir occasionally. Add salt and pepper to taste and serve cold.

Insalata di Barbabietole con Menta

BEETROOT SALAD WITH MINT

I can't stress enough that you must buy very fresh, small beetroot for this salad – ready-cooked will not do. I usually get mine in season from my garden, and they are a delicacy. The combination of fresh mint and sweet beetroot make an excellent dish that is not only a great starter but also a wonderful accompaniment to roast chicken or grilled fish.

SERVES 4

16 small fresh beetroot
20 mint leaves

DRESSING
4 tbsp extra virgin olive oil
1 tbsp white wine vinegar
salt and pepper

Cook the beetroot in plenty of boiling water until the tip of a knife enters the beetroot very easily (about 30 minutes). Drain well.

When cool enough to handle, peel the beetroot and cut into thin slices. Put in a bowl and add the mint.

For the dressing, combine the oil, vinegar, salt and pepper in a small bowl and mix well. Toss together with the beetroot and mint and serve.

Zuppe, Passati e Minestre
SOUPS

The Italians recognise several different types of soup. A *zuppa*, generally speaking, is a broth containing ingredients which have not been liquidised; a *passata* is generally a *zuppa* which has been liquidised or creamed (known as a *crema* as well); and a *minestra* is a soup usually based on broth and green vegetables. Soups can be made with anything – meat, fish or vegetables – and are often accompanied by pasta or rice for thickening or, if very liquid, by a slice of bread.

Passata Estiva di Cetrioli e Pomodori

RAW CUCUMBER AND TOMATO SUMMER SOUP

For this soup, the ingredients are raw, and the mixture of the two soups and two colours is spectacular to look at. It is a delightfully refreshing dish for a hot summer's day!

SERVES 4

1 large cucumber, peeled
  and cut into chunks
2 tbsp finely chopped dill
3 tbsp double cream
salt and pepper
2 large beef tomatoes, skinned
  (see page 43) and chopped
10 basil leaves, plus extra to garnish
1 white onion, peeled and roughly chopped

Liquidise the cucumber with the dill in a liquidiser or food processor. Add the cream and season to taste with a little salt and pepper. Chill in the fridge.

Liquidise the skinned tomatoes with the basil and onion. Season to taste and chill in the fridge.

To serve, first put the cucumber soup in a deep soup plate, then carefully add the tomato soup in the centre and garnish with a few basil leaves.

 TO MAKE IT MORE SPECIAL
For extra colour and texture, try adding a tablespoon of very finely chopped tomato and cucumber to each serving.

Pasta e Fagioli

PASTA AND BEAN SOUP

As with *minestrone* this pasta and bean soup exists in at least 20 versions, depending on the region where it originates. It is usually based on a stock flavoured by a Parma ham bone: though vegetarian versions, such as this one below, are now rather fashionable.

SERVES 6

250g dried borlotti or cannellini beans, or 3 x 400g cans unsalted borlotti beans, drained and rinsed

2 celery stalks, cubed

4 tbsp extra virgin olive oil

1 fresh red chilli, chopped

2 garlic cloves, peeled and finely chopped

3 ripe tomatoes, skinned (see page 43) and chopped, or 400g canned chopped tomatoes

1 litre vegetable stock or water

115g mixed small pasta pieces or *tubettini*

10 basil leaves, shredded

salt and pepper

If you are using dried beans, soak in water overnight, boil in unsalted water for 2-3 hours until tender, and drain.

Fry the celery in the olive oil in a large saucepan over a medium heat for a few minutes before adding the chilli.

After about 10 minutes add the garlic and cook for a couple of minutes, until soft, then add the tomatoes. Wait a further 10 minutes before adding two-thirds of the beans, keeping the remainder aside to be mashed and added to thicken the dish.

Pour in the stock or water and bring to the boil. Now add the pasta and, after 8 minutes add the basil leaves and the mashed beans. Season to taste with salt and pepper and serve.

TO MAKE IT MORE SPECIAL
When serving, amazing flavour is added with just a trickle of extra virgin olive oil on the top of each dish. If you like it, you could add some chilli oil instead. But please, don't add Parmesan.

Vellutata di Cannellini e Porcini

CEP AND CANNELLINI BEAN VELOUTÉ

The word *velouté* is borrowed from the French, which means a soup with a velvety consistency. *Passata* would be more Italian but since the French borrow Italian culinary terminology, why not the reverse? The cep or *porcino* is the king of wild mushrooms, and is available fresh only during its brief season.

SERVES 4

150g dried cannellini beans
400g small fresh porcini (ceps)
60g butter
1 whole garlic clove, peeled
salt and pepper
500ml vegetable stock
40ml double cream
50g Parmesan (optional), freshly grated

Soak the dried cannellini beans in water overnight. Drain, then add to a large saucepan, cover with fresh water, bring to the boil and cook for 10 minutes. Reduce the heat to a simmer and cook for 1½–2 hours. Drain.

Clean the porcini carefully, brushing off any dust, and checking inside the stems for any unwelcome visitors. Cut the mushrooms and stems into slices. Sauté the porcini in the butter with the garlic for 10 minutes. Remove the garlic from the pan and discard, then season to taste.

Put the stock in a pan, add the cannellini beans and porcini and cook for a few minutes. Season, then add the double cream and liquidise in a food processor to obtain a velvety consistency. Pour into serving bowls and, sprinkle with Parmesan, if desired.

ALTERNATE (CHEAPER) VERSION
In place of the porcini, cook 300g button mushrooms in the same way, then add 20g rehydrated dried porcini mushrooms (see page 102) and cook for a further 10 minutes. Season with salt and pepper, then add the stock, and process as before.

Passato di Zucca

PUMPKIN SOUP

Autumn and winter offer lots of roots and squash which can be used in soup. This type of pumpkin soup is more likely to be served in the north and especially the northeast part of Italy, from where *speck* (an air-dried and smoked shoulder of pork) originates.

SERVES 4

1 medium onion, peeled and finely chopped
2 tbsp olive oil
1 litre chicken or vegetable stock
600g pumpkin flesh, cut into cubes
200g celeriac, peeled and cut into cubes
salt and pepper

Fry the onion in the olive oil in a large saucepan until soft, but not browning, about 10 minutes.

Add the stock and, when boiling, the cubes of pumpkin and celeriac, and cook until soft, about 15–20 minutes. Add salt and pepper to taste.

Liquidise in a food processor or blender and return to the pan.
Reheat the soup and pour into serving bowls. Serve hot.

TO MAKE IT MORE SPECIAL
Cut a 50g slice of *speck* or smoked *pancetta*, 5mm thick, into strips then cubes. Heat 4 tbsp of olive oil in a frying pan, add the *speck* or *pancetta* and cook until crisp. Add 2 tbsp finely chopped rosemary and stir to combine, before spooning a quarter of the mixture into the centre of each bowl of soup.

Minestrone

THICK VEGETABLE SOUP

In Italy there are as many recipes for *minestrone* ('big *minestra*' as soups are called when based on vegetables and greens) as there are households. Depending on what is in season, or what is in the house, a *minestrone* can vary a lot, though usually it includes some beans, potatoes, tomatoes, cabbage, spinach, cauliflower, carrots, with herb flavours like basil, rosemary and even pesto.

SERVES 4

1 large onion, peeled and diced
6 tbsp olive oil
150g each of carrots and potatoes, peeled and diced
150g each of courgettes, celery and tomatoes, diced
150g fresh podded borlotti beans or peas, or cooked chickpeas
1.5 litres vegetable stock or water
2 vegetable stock cubes
10 basil leaves, shredded
salt and pepper
50g Parmesan (optional), freshly grated
extra virgin olive oil

Fry the onion in the olive oil in a large pan for about 5 minutes, then add all the diced vegetables and the beans or chickpeas. Cover with stock or water, crumble in the stock cubes, cover with the lid and leave to gently simmer for 30 minutes, until the vegetables are soft.

Add the basil and season to taste. Sprinkle with Parmesan, if desired, drizzle with extra virgin olive oil and serve.

TO MAKE IT MORE SPECIAL
The *soupe au pistou* of Provence is nothing more than a *minestrone* with the addition of *pistou*, the French version of pesto, at the end. Try this for a glorious taste. Some people add short pasta to thicken the soup, and you can use rice as well. If you want to, add 60g of either of these halfway through the simmering of the vegetables.

Ombelico di Venere in Brodo

STUFFED PASTA (VENUS'S BELLY BUTTON) IN BROTH

I tend to eat it this simple dish anywhere I can find it. The little stuffed pasta – *tortellini*, *cappelletti*, or *anolini* as they call them in Bologna – are usually hand-made, and look amazing. Although I think they look like little hats, some imaginative Italians have christened them 'Venus's belly button'. While preparing them from fresh is quite difficult, you can buy a ready-made fresh variety from good delicatessens.

SERVES 4

1 litre chicken or beef stock
salt and pepper
400g good-quality fresh *tortellini* or *cappelletti*
60g Parmesan, freshly grated

Put the stock into a pan, and boil gently until it has reduced to 600ml. This intensifies the flavour.

Bring the stock back to the boil and check for salt and pepper. Add the pasta and cook according to the instructions of the vendor or the packet, usually between 4–6 minutes (but it can vary a lot).

Spoon the stock and pasta into deep soup plates and sprinkle over the Parmesan to finish.

ALTERNATE SERVING SUGGESTION
You could cook the pasta in the stock, drain, and then fry in butter with some sage as a little pasta starter. Alternatively, you could retain a little of the stock in the frying pan, add a little double cream and some shreds of ham to create a different sauce for the pasta (making this into a dish known in Italy as *tortellini alla panna*).

Stracciatella con Gnocchetti di Pollo

EGG BROTH WITH CHICKEN DUMPLINGS

Stracciatella is a soup you can find in many old restaurants. It's basically a soup for people with small appetites, and I find it rather bland. To make it more interesting I have added some delicious chicken dumplings.

SERVES 4

1 litre very good chicken stock, boiling
2 whole eggs plus 2 egg yolks, beaten
  together
20g Parmesan, freshly grated
2 tbsp chervil leaves, chopped
salt and pepper

CHICKEN DUMPLINGS
200g minced chicken
2 egg whites, beaten stiff
30g Parmesan, freshly grated
2 tbsp very finely chopped chives

To make the dumplings, first mix the chicken mince in a bowl with the stiffly beaten egg whites, the Parmesan and chives. Season to taste with salt and abundant pepper. Using two teaspoons, shape the chicken mixture into quenelles or dumplings and plunge into the boiling stock. Cook for 8 minutes before scooping out and setting aside.

In another bowl, mix the beaten eggs and yolks with the Parmesan, chervil and salt and pepper to taste. Carefully pour this mixture into the boiling stock while whisking quickly to obtain a thickish broth.

Return the dumplings to the broth and serve immediately.

LEFTOVERS
You could use the dumplings in other ways too: you could coat them in breadcrumbs and fry them to eat as little rissoles, or cook them in a good tomato sauce made with oil, garlic, tomato *passata* and basil (or see page 69). Cooked in a sauce, they could be served as a dressing for pasta.

Zuppa di Ceci e Costine

SOUP OF SPARE RIBS
AND CHICKPEAS

This soup, which is very much loved by southern Italian farmers, is not only cheap to produce, but tasty and rewarding. The chickpeas can be from a can or a jar, thus avoiding hours of soaking and cooking. Try to find very meaty spare ribs to give this soup plenty of body.

SERVES 4

Extra virgin olive oil
800g meaty pork spare ribs, separated
2 celery stalks, finely chopped
2 garlic cloves, peeled and finely chopped
2 medium carrots, peeled and finely chopped
10 sun-dried tomatoes, finely chopped
1.5 litres water
3 x 400g cans cooked chickpeas, drained
½ fresh chilli, chopped
4 basil leaves, chopped
salt and pepper

Put 4 tbsp of the olive oil in a large saucepan and fry the spare ribs, browning each side. Keep in the pan. Add all the chopped fresh vegetables and sun-dried tomatoes and cook for a further 10 minutes.

Add the water and bring to the boil. Simmer over a medium heat for 1 hour, then scoop off and discard the fat from the top of the liquid. Add the drained chickpeas, the chilli and the basil and cook until the meat is tender, another 30–40 minutes, adding a little water if the soup looks as though it needs a little extra liquid.

Season with a little salt and pepper and pour into bowls, drizzle with a little extra virgin olive oil and serve.

Zuppa di Pesce

SIMPLE FISH SOUP

Fish soups are very regional, being made differently, often from village to village, along the coastline of Italy. In the Marche region it is called *brodetto*, 'little broth', and uses the local fresh fish. A fish soup is also classic in Venice, which incorporates various molluscs from the lagoon.

SERVES 4

6 tbsp olive oil
1 small onion, peeled and finely chopped
2–3 tbsp *passata*
1kg mussels, cleaned (see below)
300g monkfish, cut into medium cubes
300g squid, cleaned and cut into rings (see page 36)
at least 500ml good French *soupe de poissons*
  (in most supermarkets or delicatessens)
4 thick slices country bread, toasted

First of all heat the olive oil in a large saucepan and fry the onion until softened, about 6–7 minutes. Add the *passata*, and in this cook the mussels, monkfish and squid rings, for about 10 minutes. Discard any mussels that haven't opened.

Stir in your fish soup and heat through gently, about 5 minutes. Placing a slice of toasted bread at the base of each, pour the soup into bowls and serve.

CLEANING MUSSELS OR CLAMS
Cover the mussels or clams with water and scrub well to get rid of sand and barnacles. Pull and cut away any stringy beards. Discard any mussels or clams that do not close when tapped, as they are probably dead. Wash again.

Pasta
PASTA

If pasta didn't exist, it would have to be urgently invented. Italy is generally recognised as the home of pasta, and this dish is consumed and enjoyed at least once daily: there are more than 600 official shapes and an equal amount of sauce combinations. Pasta is versatile, economical, easy to prepare, satisfying, good as an energy provider and fun to eat. Enough with the praise!

Pasta is such a rich, intricate and diverse subject that it really deserves an entire book of this size all on its own. I will try with the space given here to explain the complex philosophy of pasta. For there are certain rules which, when observed, produce excellence; if they are not followed, the result is mediocrity.

TYPES OF PASTA

Most commercial pasta is made with durum (hard) wheat semolina and water. It is extruded through a machine with a die at high pressure, cut to size and dried in a process lasting some 12 hours. Other commercial, dried pastas are made with the addition of eggs. This gives more protein and a different texture.

There is also a hand-made pasta, made with just water, durum wheat semolina and 00 flour. This comes usually from Puglia where they hand-make *orrecchiette*, *fusilli*, *strozzapreti* and *cecatelli*, and also from Tuscany, where the pasta is called *strangozzi*.

Stuffed pastas are also available everywhere now, such as *ravioli*, *tortellini*, *tortelloni*, *tortelli* and *cappelletti* (very good in broth). These are best freshly made, and can be bought in good delicatessens.

For special occasions, Italians feel they must make their own fresh pasta, either simply with flour and water, or with egg. In my opinion there are very few good fresh pastas available in shops, and I firmly believe the best is one that you make yourself. If you do want to try it, see page 121 for a recipe for fresh *fusilli*.

PASTA SAUCES

RIGHT PASTA, RIGHT SAUCE

Spaghetti and all round and long pastas are suitable for most sauces, but not *bolognese*. The ideal pastas for *bolognese* are home-made egg *tagliatelle* (a flat ribbon of pasta), and dried egg and egg-less *tagliatelle* (from shops). *Tagliolini*, the smallest form of *tagliatelle*, is particularly good with truffle and other delicate sauces like crab or lobster. Angel's hair or *capelli d'angelo* is a particularly thin type of long pasta, which is wonderful with a simple tomato sauce and even in broth. Short bulky pasta like *paccheri*, *macaroni* and *penne* are good for *arrabbiata* or long-cooked meat and tomato *ragù*. The very small pasta, *pastina*, is used in broth and soups.

TOMATO PASTA SAUCES

The majority of Italian pasta sauces contains tomatoes. Besides colour, a ripe tomato gives a certain degree of acidity to balance the other ingredients, which results in a wonderful taste. Out of season (and sometimes in season too), Italians now use a great deal of canned and jarred tomato products, which are very convenient indeed.

—CANNED PEELED TOMATOES, called *pelati*, which contain the seeds, pulp and lots of water, can be used in long cooking sauces.

—CHOPPED TOMATOES IN CANS, also called tomato pulp are very useful. The pulp is in chunks, without seeds or skin, and can be used for any sort of sauce.

—TOMATO PASSATA in jars is liquidised and strained tomato, which is of a thinnish consistency (often too thin for my liking). This can be used by itself (as a sort of coulis) or in combination with the other two above for long-cooking sauces, and also for immediate use.

—TOMATO CONCENTRATE is a paste or purée (usually in a tube, sometimes a little can), which consists of a double concentration of tomato. This is used to reinforce the taste of normal tomatoes. In Sicily they use a six-times concentrate sold everywhere called *strattu*, from 'extract'. It is solid, very dark in colour and has to be diluted with water.

OTHER PASTA SAUCES

—MEATS are often used in sauces. Minced beef, veal, pork or even game like wild boar, deer, hare and pheasant etc, are used for *ragù* (long-cooked sauces). Sometimes chicken livers and sweetbreads are added. Cured and preserved meats (*speck*, smoked ham, *pancetta*, Parma ham, *salami*) are also great flavour additions.

—ALL TYPES OF SEAFOOD, like mussels, clams, lobster, crab, scallops, prawns, shrimps, cuttlefish, squid, octopus, and many de-boned fish such as red mullet, monkfish, sardines, tuna and even Dover sole, are used in a number of popular pasta sauces. Canned or jarred anchovies, either preserved in salt or oil, are particularly important.

—VEGETABLES such as broccoli, cauliflower, chicory, green beans, broad beans, peas, artichokes, asparagus, borlotti and cannellini beans, potatoes, spinach, pumpkin, beetroot, chickpeas and mushrooms add texture and flavour to pasta sauces. Onion and garlic (sometimes together) are basics, as are carrot and celery (all forming part of what the Italians call *soffritto*). Dried porcini mushrooms (ceps) are wonderful when the fresh are not available.

—FLAVOURINGS AND CONDIMENTS vary enormously. Olive oil, butter or both together, are vital, as are salt and pepper, eggs on occasion, and truffle oil every now and then. I'm not fond of cream with pasta unless I am making *tortellini* with cream and ham, as I find it reduces everything to the same taste. Wine and vinegar play a part, as do the great cheeses of Italy – Parmesan and grana padano, Fontina, Gorgonzola, pecorino, mozzarella and Taleggio.

—A lack of success in pasta sauces is often due to the wrong use of herbs. Italians don't use them too profligately, just appropriately to the dish. Celery leaves, basil, parsley (flat-leaf), chives, chervil, rosemary, fresh oregano (very strong), mint, rocket and chillies are used often, but with care and love.

Whatever you choose, do remember that in Italy generally the simpler the better.

PASTA COOKING AND EATING

— The pot for boiling the pasta must be high and large.

— Use 1 litre of water for 100g pasta.

— For small portions, allow 50g of pasta per person; 70–80g for normal portions and 100–110g for large portions.

— Add 10g salt per litre to the water just before boiling.

— Place the pasta into the boiling water and stir after 20–30 seconds.

— Don't add oil unless you are cooking pasta sheets like *lasagne*.

— Cook for from 2–3 minutes for fresh home-made pasta up to 18–20 minutes for dried non-egg pasta (follow the directions on the packet).

— For soups or minestrones put the pasta directly in the stock.

— Test one piece of pasta towards the end of cooking to see if it is to your liking. The Italians like it cooked, but still with a light resistance to the tooth (*al dente*).

— Have the sauce prepared, and place a few tablespoons in a hot soup bowl.

— Drain the pasta, but do not wash under cold water, and mix with a little of the sauce. (The sauce might benefit from a few tablespoons of the pasta cooking water if it is too thick.)

— Place portions in hot plates, and top up with more sauce. But remember, the pasta mustn't be swimming in sauce.

— If necessary add freshly grated Parmesan or pecorino cheese. Pasta with fish sauce is better tossed with the sauce in the pan (and no Parmesan added).

— Serve the pasta hot, and if it is long, eat only with a fork: lift a few strings of pasta from the plate, make a little space on the side, pin the fork down and start to twirl. This is to avoid too big a morsel. Try also not to suck strings into your mouth (although this is permitted for babies). Eat only soupy pasta with a spoon. This is the be-all and end-all of pasta etiquette!

Spaghetti Aglio, Olio e Peperoncino

SPAGHETTI WITH GARLIC, OIL AND CHILLI

This is probably one of the most popular recipes for native Italians. They like to eat it at any time, but it's probably the prime dish to be eaten for a midnight feast, when they arrive home late and hungry. It takes only about 6–7 minutes to cook the pasta, while the 'sauce' is ready in less than half that time. You don't even have to grate any Parmesan, as the pasta is better without it.

SERVES 2 (MULTIPLY AS NEEDED)

salt
180g *spaghetti*

SAUCE
2 garlic cloves, peeled and finely chopped
1 small red chilli, finely chopped
6 tbsp olive oil

Put plenty of water in a saucepan, add salt, bring to the boil and throw in the pasta. Stir, then cook for about 5–6 minutes, until nearly done.

Now start the sauce by heating the olive oil gently in a deep frying pan. Add the garlic and chilli and fry for a few seconds, or until the garlic starts to change colour. Take care not to burn the garlic.

The pasta will be ready and *al dente* in those few minutes. Drain it well and put in the pan with the 'sauce', adding a little salt and perhaps 1–2 tbsp of the pasta cooking water. Stir a couple of times and serve.

TO MAKE IT MORE SPECIAL
For people who think this is too simple, you could add a further burst of flavour by including a couple of anchovy fillets. Fry them along with the garlic and chilli, and they will melt into the oil. You could add a teaspoon of tiny capers too if you liked, or some very finely cubed green olives. Or, at the end, you could grate some *bottarga* (dried and salted tuna or grey mullet roe) over the top of each portion.

Rigatoni alla Giardiniera con Polpettine di Spinaci

PASTA WITH COURGETTE SAUCE AND SPINACH BALLS

This is a recipe I created for Carluccio's Caffès. It is still on the menu, and every time someone orders it, some money goes to charity. It has proved so popular that Carluccio's was able to collect £70,000 in just three months!

SERVES 4

1 recipe spinach balls (see page 24)
400g *rigatoni* (large ridged pasta tubes)
salt and pepper

SAUCE
2 garlic cloves, peeled and finely chopped
1 chilli, finely chopped
8 tbsp olive oil
2 courgettes, trimmed and finely grated
60g Parmesan, freshly grated

Prepare the spinach balls in advance and keep warm in a very low oven.

In a saucepan of boiling salted water, cook the pasta until *al dente*, about 8–10 minutes. When ready, drain, reserving a few tablespoons of the pasta cooking water.

Meanwhile, make the sauce. Fry the garlic and chilli in the oil for about a minute – don't let the garlic brown – then add the courgettes, and cook for about 3–4 minutes, until the courgettes have started to soften.

Add the Parmesan to the sauce, season to taste and mix well, then toss thoroughly with the drained pasta and reserved cooking water. Serve hot with the warmed spinach balls on top.

Pappardelle con Frittedda

WIDE PASTA RIBBONS WITH SPRINGTIME SAUCE

Frittedda, in the Sicilian dialect, means a stew of asparagus, young onions, small broad beans, peas and artichokes, all of which are in season between March and April. It makes an excellent sauce for the largest size of pasta ribbon, *pappardelle*.

SERVES 4–6

350g *pappardelle*
salt and pepper
freshly grated Parmesan (optional)

SAUCE
8 small artichokes
300g asparagus
300g white young onions, peeled and finely sliced
300g podded tender broad beans
200g podded tender garden peas
6 tbsp olive oil
100ml water
3 tbsp coarsely chopped parsley

To make the sauce, first prepare the artichokes by removing the tough outer leaves and trim the base of the stems. With a sharp knife, trim the tips of the leaves, leaving only the tender parts. Cut into quarters and remove any choke.

Put all the vegetables in a large saucepan with the oil and water. Cook gently for 20 minutes then, when you are sure everything is cooked, add some salt and pepper and the parsley. Mix well.

In a saucepan of boiling salted water, cook the pasta until *al dente*, about 7–8 minutes. Drain and mix with the sauce. Sprinkle with Parmesan cheese, if desired, and serve.

Pasta Imbottita con Vegetali al Forno

RICH OVEN-BAKED VEGETABLE PASTA

Not long ago I had the enviable task of cooking a famous timbale for a BBC TV documentary about the Sicilian Principe di Salina, Tomasi di Lampedusa (*Il Gattopardo* or The Leopard). The historical recipe turned out to be a triumph, but was a little too elaborate for this book. So I have devised this pasta dish instead, which requires a little bit of work and should probably be made for celebrations and special occasions. To make life simpler you can prepare it the day before serving.

SERVES 8–10

600g large *rigatoni*
salt and pepper

TOMATO SAUCE
2 large onions, peeled and finely chopped
100ml olive oil
1.5kg tomato pulp (*polpa di pomodoro*)
  or canned chopped tomatoes
10 basil leaves, shredded

FILLING
2 aubergines, cut in 8mm thick slices lengthways
2 courgettes, cut in 8mm thick slices lengthways
plain flour, to dust
6 eggs
olive oil, for shallow-frying
1 recipe spinach balls (see page 24)
8 whole baby courgettes, trimmed
2 fennel bulbs, trimmed
600g melting cheese, like Fontina, Bel Paese,
  Taleggio, cut into little chunks
200g Parmesan, freshly grated

Bigoli in Salsa di Cipolle e Acciughe

GIANT SPAGHETTI WITH ONION AND ANCHOVY SAUCE

This is a Venetian speciality, and is very easy to make. In the Veneto, people still make the special pasta by hand with the help of a little implement – a *torcolo* – which has a chamber through which the pasta is pushed. This produces a thick spaghetti with a 4mm diameter and no hole. The alternative is *bucatini*, which is the same size, but has a little hole inside.

SERVES 4

400g *bigoli* or *bucatini*
salt and pepper

SAUCE
600g onions, peeled and finely chopped
6 tbsp olive oil
40g anchovy fillets in oil

For the sauce, fry the onion in a pan with the olive oil until soft, about 6–7 minutes, then add the anchovies, which will dissolve in the heat. Stir them in very briefly.

Cook the pasta in plenty of boiling salted water until *al dente*, probably about 8–9 minutes. Drain and mix into the sauce. Season with a little salt and plenty of pepper. Mix well and serve hot.

TO MAKE IT MORE SPECIAL
If you are feeling greedy and want to give this sauce a little more substance, try adding 150g tuna flakes in oil, drained, once you have fried the onions until soft.

Spaghetti alla Carrettiera

CART-DRIVER SPAGHETTI

This recipe goes back to the time when the agricultural people from the country drove into town in carts pulled by horses and donkeys. The driver knew how to cook something unusual and extremely tasty for himself when he reached his destination.

SERVES 2 (CAN BE MULTIPLIED)

200g *spaghetti*
salt and pepper

SAUCE
1 small onion, peeled and finely sliced
4 tbsp olive oil
2 ripe tomatoes, finely chopped
25g dried porcini (ceps), rehydrated
  (see page 102) and finely sliced
100g canned tuna in oil, drained

For the sauce, fry the onion in a pan with the olive oil until soft, about 5–6 minutes, then add the tomatoes and fry for 15 minutes. Add the sliced porcini and some of their liquid, along with the tuna and some salt and pepper to taste.

Cook the pasta in plenty of boiling salted water until *al dente*, about 5–6 minutes. Drain, mix with the sauce and serve immediately.

Capelli D'Angelo Neri con Capesante e Gamberetti

BLACK ANGEL'S HAIR PASTA WITH SCALLOPS AND SHRIMPS

I had the good fortune in Italy to find small black *spaghettini*, almost as fine as angel's hair. This type of pasta is made by incorporating the black ink of cuttlefish, and is very typical of Venice. If you can't find this pasta, you can substitute black *tagliatelle*. The other alternative is to buy normal *spaghettini* and add the black ink (which is fairly readily available in good delicatessens) to the sauce.

SERVES 4

400g black *spaghettini* or *tagliatelle*
salt and pepper
a little extra virgin olive oil

SAUCE
4 tbsp olive oil
2 garlic cloves, peeled and finely
  chopped

1 small red chilli, finely chopped
8 large shelled scallops with corals
200g cooked pink shrimps, shelled
50ml dry white wine
2 tbsp coarsely chopped flat-leaf
  parsley

While you cook the pasta in plenty of boiling salted water as usual, until *al dente*, about 4–5 minutes, you have time to make the sauce.

Put the olive oil, garlic and chilli in a large frying pan and fry briefly until the garlic has softened. Add the scallops, shrimps and wine, and fry for a further 2 minutes. Add the parsley, salt and pepper to taste, and the sauce is ready.

Drain the pasta, add to the sauce, mix well and divide between the plates, finishing each with a drizzle of extra virgin olive oil.

Linguine Vongole e Cozze

LINGUINE WITH CLAMS AND MUSSELS

You will find this dish in all the coastal towns and villages, most famously in the *laguna* of Venice. It is the seafood pasta 'par excellence'. There exist two versions of the sauce: *in rosso* (with tomatoes) or *in bianco* (without tomatoes). I prefer the second, featured here, as you can appreciate the taste of the seafood much more easily.

SERVES 4

400g *linguine*
salt and pepper
1 bunch flat-leaf parsley, finely
  chopped
extra virgin olive oil

SAUCE
1kg mussels, cleaned (see page 58)
1kg small clams, cleaned (see page 58)
6 tbsp olive oil
100ml dry white wine
2 garlic cloves, peeled and finely diced
1 small red chilli (optional), chopped

For the sauce, put the mussels and clams in a large saucepan with the olive oil, wine, garlic and chilli (if using). Bring to the boil with the lid on and cook for a further 10 minutes before removing from the heat. Discard any mussels that haven't opened. Remove the meat from the shells (reserving a few for garnish) and keep to one side. Discard the empty shells.

At the base of the pan will be the sauce made of oil, wine, juices from the shells, garlic and chilli, if desired. Keep this warm.

In a separate pan, cook the pasta in plenty of boiling salted water until *al dente*, about 6–7 minutes. Drain and add to the sauce. Add salt, lots of pepper and the parsley, along with the shellfish flesh.

Divide between the plates, adding a few drops of extra virgin olive oil and the few remaining shell-on fish. Serve immediately.

 CHEESE WITH SEAFOOD PASTA
The Italians would only use cheese with seafood when baking or grilling it – with lobster or crab, say, cooked under the grill. Otherwise they believe the cheese spoils the fresh flavour of the sea, and does not complement it at all.

orecchiette Baresi con Broccoli e Cozze

EAR-SHAPED PASTA WITH BROCCOLI AND MUSSELS

This is a typical Pugliese coastal dish, from Bari, which was originally accompanied by what is known as *cime di rape*, or rape tops. These are not generally available outside Italy, and the easiest alternative is little tips of broccoli (the calabrese type) or purple sprouting broccoli. Instead of *orrechiette* you could try this recipe with *gnocchetti sardi* or *penne*.

SERVES 4–6

350g *orecchiette pugliesi*
salt and pepper

SAUCE
300g small broccoli florets
6 tbsp olive oil
2 garlic cloves, peeled and finely sliced
1 small chilli, chopped
200g cherry tomatoes, halved
800g mussels, cleaned (see page 58)

For the sauce, boil the florets in salted water until al dente, about 8–9 minutes. Drain.

Using a large frying pan with a lid, add the olive oil, garlic, chilli and tomatoes. Fry briefly, until the garlic has softened, then add the mussels and cover with the lid. Continue to cook until the mussels have opened, about 10 minutes. Discard any that have not opened, and most of the shells, saving the mussel meat in the sauce.

Add the cooked broccoli florets and heat up to allow the broccoli to absorb the flavours.

Cook the pasta in plenty of boiling salted water until *al dente*, about 10–12 minutes. Drain well and mix with the sauce. Season with a little salt and lots of pepper and serve in deep plates.

Gnocchi, polenta e riso
GNOCCHI, POLENTA & RICE

Pasta and bread are the primary carbohydrate foods in Italian cuisine, but not far behind come gnocchi, polenta and rice. The first are dumplings usually made from potato, the second are made from a variety of grains and pulses, while the third is a grain that can be used to create one of the most unique and famous of all Italian dishes, risotto.

All can be presented and flavoured in different ways, and help introduce a little welcome variety into the typical Italian diet.

GNOCCHI

A variety of gnocchi exist, but the simplest and most widely encountered are those made with mashed potatoes and a little flour. To make them is simplicity itself. For a serving for four people, cook and mash 400g of floury potatoes, then mix with 100g of plain flour and an egg. Using your hands, roll a little of this mixture at a time into sausage shapes. Cut these into 3cm chunks, then press with the tines of a fork to create a ridged impression (these ridges will help the sauce to stick). Add the gnocchi to boiling salted water, after a few seconds they will swim up to the surface. Scoop them out before dressing immediately with your chosen sauce.

Green gnocchi are made by adding a little cooked, well-drained and very finely chopped spinach. Another type of gnocchi is what is known as *gnocchi alla romana*, and these are made with semolina or polenta. This is boiled in milk, mixed with egg and nutmeg then cut out and layered in a dish, before being baked with butter and Parmesan.

Gnocchi di Patate al Gorgonzola

POTATO DUMPLINGS
WITH GORGONZOLA SAUCE

Gnocchi are very moreish. Light and fluffy, it won't matter how many you have in front of you – you will eat them all. The primary thing to remember is that the potato should be fresh, not cooked in advance, which can make the gnocchi rubbery and leaden.

SERVES 4

1 recipe potato gnocchi (see left)
salt and pepper
60g Parmesan, freshly grated

SAUCE
60g unsalted butter
50g Gorgonzola or Dolcelatte cheese, in chunks
a little double cream as required

Make the gnocchi as described opposite.

Meanwhile, make the sauce. Melt the butter in a pan and add the Gorgonzola or Dolcelatte. Break the cheese up with a fork and add enough cream to give the sauce the desired smooth, rich consistency.

Add the cooked gnocchi to the sauce, season with salt and pepper and sprinkle with Parmesan. Serve immediately.

TO MAKE IT MORE SPECIAL
Wash and dry a few baby spinach leaves (about 10 per person). Put in a pan with a tablespoon of water and a touch of olive oil, cover and heat until the leaves have wilted, a few seconds only. Stir into the sauce.

Gnocchi Verdi al Pomodoro e Mozzarella

GREEN GNOCCHI WITH TOMATO AND MOZZARELLA

In a way this simple, yet delicious dish can be seen to represent the colours of the Italian flag – green, red and white.

SERVES 4

500g mashed floury potatoes
110g plain flour
200g spinach, cooked and squeezed dry (see page 24)
  and very finely chopped
1 egg
salt and pepper
40g Parmesan, freshly grated
150g buffalo mozzarella, cut into small cubes

TOMATO SAUCE
1 garlic clove, peeled and finely chopped
6 tbsp olive oil
500g canned chopped tomatoes
6 basil leaves

Make the gnocchi by mixing together the potatoes, flour, spinach and egg, adding more flour if the dough is too wet. Season lightly.

Make the simple tomato sauce by frying the garlic in the olive oil until soft, a few minutes. Add the tomatoes, basil, and some salt and pepper, and cook for 20 minutes.

Cook the gnocchi as per the recipe on page 90. When ready, drain, then add the sauce, Parmesan and some pepper, and mix well.

Divide the gnocchi between the plates, sprinkling over the mozzarella cubes and some more basil leaves to finish.

POLENTA

Polenta is the name for a maize or corn flour, and for the dishes made from it. Maize reached Europe via Spain, imported from the Americas following the great discoveries of the sixteenth century. Easy to cultivate, and cropping well, it was immediately adopted by the Italians, especially in the north where the growing conditions were optimal.

After a long period out of fashion – it was seen as a food of poverty for many decades – polenta has made a comeback in home cooking as well as in good restaurants, where it is offered with all sorts of sauces. It used to be quite a job cooking polenta because it takes about 40 minutes of stirring. Now however, a pre-cooked 'quick' polenta has been developed, which takes only 5 minutes to cook. Although in my opinion this is not as tasty as the original, it is quite acceptable.

Polenta has various functions, mostly as an accompaniment to a sauce or stew, which could be of chicken, rabbit or sausages, or wild mushrooms (or a mixture). It can be eaten fresh, with the addition of grated Parmesan and butter, which changes the texture, making it ideal to accompany roasts instead of mashed potato. It can also be cooked fresh and then left to solidify, after which it can be cut in slices and fried or grilled to make the perfect accompaniment for any meat or vegetable.

Polenta Svelta con Gamberetti

QUICK POLENTA WITH SHRIMPS

A delightful and simple little dish from Venice, where the little pink shrimps of the lagoon taste very nice indeed.

SERVES 4

1 litre water
salt
200g quick polenta
120g Parmesan, freshly grated
100g unsalted butter

SAUCE
300g pink shrimps, shelled
50g unsalted butter
juice of 2 lemons

In a saucepan, bring the water to the boil with some salt and add the polenta slowly, stirring well, so that you don't produce lumps. After 5 minutes add the Parmesan and butter, and mix well.

In another pan, gently fry the shrimps in the butter for 5 minutes, before adding the lemon juice.

Pour the polenta on to plates, spooning the shrimp sauce over the top.

LEFTOVERS

Obviously, if you have any leftover polenta, it will set, and you can then use it in any number of ways – cut into slices then fried or grilled to accompany anything you like. One of my friends likes it at breakfast with bacon and tomatoes! In the Aosta Valley, they break it into pieces into hot milk, and eat it like porridge, often with sugar!

Polenta Concia con Ragù di Pollo e Salsiccia

POLENTA WITH CHICKEN AND SAUSAGE STEW

I have very fond memories of Nina Burgai of the Aosta Valley, who used to have a hotel above Champorcher that could only be reached by a funicular railway, as it was 2,000 metres high. Whenever you went there she would be making a rich yet delicious polenta – this is the recipe she taught me.

SERVES 4

1.5 litres water
salt and pepper
300g quick polenta
150g Fontina cheese, cut into cubes
150g unsalted butter
150g Parmesan, freshly grated

CHICKEN AND SAUSAGE STEW
1 large onion, peeled and finely chopped

8 tbsp olive oil
400g chicken meat, in chunks
200g *luganica* sausage, skinned, or home-made sausage (see page 114) in little chunks
100ml dry white wine
800g canned chopped tomatoes

Bring the water to the boil with a little salt added. Pour the polenta in slowly and cook, stirring, until thickened and smooth, about 5–6 minutes. Add the Fontina cubes, butter and Parmesan and stir to combine.

In another pan, fry the onion in olive oil until soft, about 5 minutes, then add the chicken and sausage pieces. Allow to brown slightly, then add the wine and some salt and pepper. Cook for 5 minutes then add the tomatoes and cook until everything is tender, about 20 minutes.

Spoon the polenta and *ragù* on to the same plate, and enjoy!

RICE

Rice has only been established in Italy for 400 or 500 years. Introduced by the Arabs, it quickly became a welcome alternative to the wheat grain used for bread and pasta. Funnily enough, its cultivation started in the south of the country, where water was never going to be found in the quantities needed for the grain to grow happily. Since then production has moved to the northern regions of Piedmont, Lombardy and Veneto, where a supply of abundant water from the Alps has created the perfect conditions for growing the grain.

The Italians developed, from the original 'Japonica', the type of rice they wanted for risottos: a grain that was able to absorb enough water while cooking without falling apart, yet still remaining to the tooth (*al dente*). Various kinds of rice are produced in the Po Valley, from Vercelli in Piedmont to Venice in Veneto. The best rice for risotto are *arborio*, *vialone nano*, *Roma* and *carnaroli*. Anything else will not do!

Risotto Milanese

RISOTTO WITH SAFFRON

This is a classic dish symbolising its region – in this case Lombardy, the region most associated with rice. Saffron is always included and sometimes bone marrow. If you omit the saffron, you will have the most basic of risottos.

SERVES 4

2.5 litres chicken or vegetable stock
2g saffron strands
100g unsalted butter
1 large onion, peeled and finely
  chopped

100ml dry white wine
500g *arborio* risotto rice
salt and pepper
60g Parmesan, freshly grated

Bring the stock to the boil in a pan and keep it at a low simmer.

In a dry frying pan, toast the saffron strands for a few seconds, being careful not to burn them.

Melt 50g of the butter in a large saucepan over a low heat and fry the onion until soft, about 10 minutes. Add the wine and let it evaporate, about 2–3 minutes. Add the rice and stir to coat with the butter for a minute, then start to add the hot stock, ladle by ladle. Avoid drowning the rice in stock and wait until each ladleful is absorbed before you add the next. After 10 minutes' cooking and stirring, add the saffron and some salt and pepper. Continue to cook and add stock in the same way until the rice is *al dente*, another 8–10 minutes, then add the rest of the butter and half the grated Parmesan.

Stir well and serve, sprinkling the remaining Parmesan on top.

TO MAKE IT MORE SPECIAL
Adding 300g *luganica* sausage makes this delicate risotto more substantial. *Luganica* is a fresh pork sausage, which is made in a very long intestine 3cm in diameter. Skin the sausages and crumble them into smallish pieces. Add to the onion after 5 minutes, and cook to brown for another 5 minutes, turning frequently. Then continue as above.If you can't find luganica sausage, you could used freshly minced pork instead, so long as you season it well (see page 114).

TO REHYDRATE DRIED PORCINI (CEPS)
Soak dried porcini in water to cover for about 20 minutes. Pick the mushrooms out of the water into a sieve over a bowl. Then very carefully strain the water, preferably through muslin, into a jug or bowl. This will remove any dust that may have come off the mushrooms. The liquid will taste intensely mushroomy, and can be used in addition to the stock to add extra mushroom flavour to this risotto.

Risotto con Funghi

RISOTTO WITH MUSHROOMS

Perhaps together with risotto with truffles, risotto with ceps is the best-known of Italian rice dishes. Italians eat this only in season when the *porcino* (*Boletus edulis* or cep) is around, but the following recipe I have devised will enable you to enjoy a mushroom risotto throughout the year. Should you manage to find some fresh porcini, however, I urge you to try them, the taste is sensational!

SERVES 4

2 litres chicken or vegetable stock
4 tbsp olive oil or 50g unsalted butter
1 onion, peeled and very finely chopped
300g firm button mushrooms, finely sliced
50g dried porcini (ceps), rehydrated (see left) and chopped
350g *carnaroli* or *arborio* risotto rice
60g Parmesan, freshly grated
80g unsalted butter
salt and pepper

Put the stock in a pan, bring to the boil and keep at a low simmer.

Heat the olive oil or butter in a large pan over a low heat, add the onion and fry until soft, about 10 minutes. Add the button mushrooms and the porcini and cook for 5 minutes, until soft and lightly browned

Add the rice and stir for a minute or two, then add one or two ladles of boiling stock. Stir continuously over the heat, adding stock a ladleful at a time as each addition is absorbed. After 18–20 minutes, check for the required *al dente* texture – the rice should be tender, but with a firm bite in the centre, and the risotto should be moist.

Remove the pan from the heat, add the Parmesan and butter and stir in well. Season to taste and serve on warm plates. *Buon appetito.*

Arancini di Riso

LITTLE RICE BALLS

This is a Sicilian speciality, which is offered in bars and cafés as a small meal or snack. The rice is usually cooked specifically, and two versions are commonly offered, one filled with meat *ragù*, another with butter and mozzarella. They are the size of an orange, which is why they have the name *arancini* (little oranges). The fashion has spread all over Italy and abroad as well. This version of mine can be made with leftover risotto, even a black risotto made with cuttlefish ink. Made in smaller sizes, as here, they are ideal for party finger food.

MAKES 24 RICE BALLS

400g leftover risotto of any kind
4 eggs, beaten
salt and pepper
freshly grated nutmeg
50g Parmesan, freshly grated
100g dried white breadcrumbs (see page 33)
vegetable oil, for shallow- or deep-frying

Put the leftover risotto in a bowl, and add half of the egg mixture, some

salt, pepper, a pinch of nutmeg and Parmesan. Mix well with wet hands, then shape into apricot-sized balls.

Place the remaining beaten egg on one plate and the breadcrumbs on another. Roll the rice balls first in the egg, then in the breadcrumbs, then shallow- or deep-fry in hot oil on all sides until golden, about 5 minutes or so. Drain on kitchen paper, and serve warm or cold.

Risotto al Burro e Tartufo

TRUFFLE RISOTTO

The simplest and most sophisticated dish ever, which can be sublime with the fresh Alba truffle when in season, but can also be made with the much more economical black truffle, or even just with truffle butter and some summer truffle for decoration.

SERVES 4

80g truffle butter
2 litres good chicken, beef or vegetable stock
1 large onion, peeled and very finely chopped
50ml dry white wine
350g *carnaroli* or *arborio* risotto rice
30g unsalted butter
80g Parmesan, freshly grated
salt and pepper
1 x 60g black or white truffle

Bring the stock to the boil in a pan and keep it at a low simmer.

In a large shallow pan, melt the truffle butter and fry the onion until soft, about 7 minutes. Add the wine and let it evaporate, then add the rice and stir for a minute. Add the hot stock, ladle by ladle, adding more as it is absorbed by the rice.

After 18–20 minutes, taste a grain to see if it is *al dente*. At this point, take the risotto off the heat and stir in the butter and Parmesan. Season to taste.

Serve with the truffle thinly sliced on top of each portion.

TRUFFLE BUTTER
You can buy this in a jar in good delicatessens. It is a wonderful ingredient to have handy, and tastes delicious. I love to fry eggs in it (and of course a truffle kept near new-laid eggs magically imbues them with its fragrance)! An alternative would be to use normal butter with the addition of a few drops of truffle oil.

Risotto alla Marinara

SEAFOOD RISOTTO

This risotto, with its base of poached, boned red mullet and lemon sole has a lovely, creamy texture. It is quite a work-intensive recipe but it is really worth it! I have chosen to use *vialone nano* rice for this dish. It is short-grained and very absorbent, which makes the risotto much tastier.

SERVES 4–6

1 large onion, peeled and finely sliced
6 tbsp olive oil
20 mussels, cleaned (see page 58)
150ml white wine
100g scampi or large prawns, shelled
100g baby octopus or squid
170g cooked shrimps, shelled
500g *vialone nano* risotto rice
extra virgin olive oil
juice of 1 lemon

FISH STOCK
1.5 litres water
1 small onion, peeled
1 carrot
a few celery and parsley leaves
2 red mullet, about 150g each
1 lemon sole, about 300g

Bring the water for the stock to the boil with the onion, carrot, celery and parsley leaves and boil for 15 minutes. Add the red mullet and sole and poach gently for a further 10 minutes. Remove the fish from the stock and fillet, discarding the bones, heads and skin. Set the fish flesh aside. Remove the flavourings from the fish stock and keep at a simmer.

Fry the onion in a large pan in the olive oil until soft, about 5 minutes. Add the mussels and the wine, cover and steam for a few minutes until the mussels open. Remove the mussels from the pan, discarding any that remain closed. Working quickly, extract the mussel meat from the shells. Reserve the meat and a few shells for decoration, discarding the rest.

To the same pan add the scampi, octopus or squid, shrimps and the reserved fish flesh and mussel meat. Add the rice, stirring so that it is coated with the oil. Add the simmering stock, ladle by ladle, as it is absorbed by the rice. The rice should be cooked in about 20–25 minutes.

Serve with a little extra virgin olive oil and a few drops of lemon juice.

Carne
MEAT

In general Italy is not a nation of carnivores. The average Italian meal, generally consisting of anything from three to five courses, rarely includes large quantities of meat – with the Italians often just as happy to eat a nice dish of well cooked and presented vegetables as something meaty. The exception to the rule is the Tuscan speciality of *bistecca alla fiorentina*, a T-bone steak of massive proportions.

The most important element when buying meat is the quality. Find yourself a trusted butcher's who supply good, fresh meat from reliable sources and are able to suggest the right meat/cut for the right dish. If you are lucky, you may also be able to pick up some cooking tips from them too!

Pollo al Rosmarino e Aglio

CHICKEN BAKED WITH ROSEMARY AND GARLIC

Needless to say, for this dish I would use one of those chickens which has lived in the courtyard and eaten the odd seed and piece of corn scratched out of the soil – naturally free-range. Italians like this simple dish, which is good hot or cold.

SERVES 4

1 x 2kg good chicken
8 garlic heads, whole
2 sprigs rosemary
6 tbsp olive oil
salt and pepper
150ml dry white wine

Preheat the oven to 200°C/Gas 6. Put the chicken into a casserole or baking tray. Add the garlic and rosemary and then pour in the olive oil. Sprinkle with salt and pepper to taste, then mix with your hands to coat everything well with oil.

Put into the preheated oven and bake for 1½ hours. Halfway through this cooking time, pour in the wine and mix well.

Continue to the end of the cooking time, remove from the oven and serve with spinach or a green salad.

LEFTOVERS
Use any leftover meat you can strip from the chicken carcass to make the chicken dumplings for a *Stracciatella con Gnochetti di Pollo* (see page 56).

Salsicce Fatte A Mano Con Lenticchie

UMBRIAN LENTIL AND HOME-MADE SAUSAGE STEW

This dish is truly wonderful when using the fresh sausages made by the local Norcian master butchers, who are known as *norcini*. As they may be difficult to find, I suggest making the sausages from scratch instead – it's not too complicated, and it is well worth it. You can get hold of Castelluccio lentils, the Italian Puy lentils, in a good delicatessen.

SERVES 4

2 garlic cloves, peeled and squashed
50g sun-dried tomatoes, cut into strips
7 tbsp extra virgin olive oil
250g Castelluccio lentils
450ml chicken stock
2 celery stalks, with leaves, chopped
salt and pepper

SAUSAGES
500g minced pork
50ml strong red wine
1 tsp fennel seeds
1 mild chilli, finely chopped
1 tsp chopped rosemary
salt and pepper

For the lentils, fry the garlic and the sun-dried tomatoes in 6 tbsp of the olive oil for a few minutes in a large pan. When the garlic starts to turn pale golden, add the lentils, stock and celery, and cook for 30 minutes or until the lentils are soft. Cover and keep warm over a low heat.

Meanwhile, in a medium-sized bowl, mix the sausage ingredients together well and season with salt and pepper. Take a handful of mince and roll it into a sausage shape, 8cm long and 3cm in diameter. Wrap tightly in a piece of foil, closing by turning the ends as you would a sweet.

Bring a large pan of water to the boil. Poach the sausages in the boiling water until they pop up to the surface, about 2–3 minutes. Leave to cool a little, then take off the foil. This poaching should ensure that the sausages hold together.

Moisten the sausages with the remaining olive oil, then fry or grill (or roast) until golden on all sides, about 5 minutes.

Add the sausages to the warm lentils, and allow to cook gently together for 5 minutes. Eat with bread or, if you like, with a few boiled potatoes.

TO MAKE IT MORE SPECIAL
These home-made sausages can be made with many different meats and spices. Replacing the pork with lamb and the fennel seeds, chilli and rosemary with 1 tsp each of chopped cumin, thyme and sage makes for a tasty alternative combination.

Costoletta di Maiale alla Milanese

MILANESE BREADED PORK CUTLET WITH BROCCOLI

Meat cooked the Milanese way is almost always breaded and fried. The most typical example is usually made with veal, but the dish is also possible with chicken or pork. For this one here, you need a large pork cutlet with the bone, the flesh beaten quite thinly. The rest is child's play.

SERVES 4

4 large pork cutlets, bone in
2 eggs, beaten with some salt and pepper
about 6 tbsp dried white breadcrumbs (see page 33)
plenty of olive oil and vegetable oil, for shallow-frying
500g purple sprouting broccoli
2 garlic cloves, peeled and sliced
½ chilli, chopped
1 lemon, quartered

Place the cutlets on a piece of clingfilm or greaseproof paper, and cover with another piece. Beat the fleshy parts with a mallet or something heavy. You want the meat to spread and become a little thinner. Remove the film or paper.

Dip the cutlets in the beaten eggs, then coat with breadcrumbs.

Pour enough mixed oil into a large shallow pan to cover the base. Heat it until it starts to bubble, then fry the cutlets on a medium-high heat for at least 5 minutes on each side until golden brown. Set aside and keep warm.

Blanch the sprouting broccoli in a pan of boiling water for a few minutes before gently frying in a pan with the sliced garlic, chopped chilli and a little olive oil until softened. Serve with the cutlets and the lemon quarters.

Tagliata di Manzo

SLICED BEEF

This dish reminds me of Tuscany where the good local meat of the Val di Chiana, a valley near Florence, makes very worthwhile eating. It is important here that you do not overcook the meat, as you want it to retain all of its natural succulence.

SERVES 4

8 tbsp olive oil, for shallow-frying
4 topside steaks, about 200g each
salt

SAUCE
12 tbsp extra virgin olive oil
2 tbsp green peppercorns
4 sprigs rosemary, divided into smaller sprigs

Pour enough olive oil into your frying pan to cover the base generously, and heat gently. Salt the steaks, add to the pan and shallow-fry for 5 minutes on each side, until browned but still rare.

In a separate small pan, warm up the extra virgin olive oil, peppercorns and rosemary over a low heat.

To serve, cut the steaks into 2cm strips. Arrange the steak slices onto four plates and drizzle over the peppery rosemary oil. *Buon appetito*.

Ragù Napoletano con Braciola

NEAPOLITAN BEEF OLIVE STEW

This classic Sunday dish of the Neapolitans is a *piatto unico* — an all-in-one dish that is served as a main course. The *braciola* is a sort of beef olive with a special filling, reminiscent of Arab cooking. These are relatively complicated to produce, but on Sundays everybody has time to prepare something so delicious.

Neapolitans make home-made *fusilli* to accompany their beef olives, and I think my old nanny Lina used to make the best.

SERVES 4–6

6 beef escalopes, quite thinly cut
3 tbsp fresh white breadcrumbs
40g raisins, soaked in water and drained
80g pine kernels
1 garlic clove, peeled and puréed
100g Parmesan, freshly grated
4 tbsp coarsely chopped flat-leaf parsley
salt and pepper

PASTA
500g durum wheat flour, plus extra to dust
1 egg, beaten

SAUCE
2 large onions, peeled and sliced
about 6 tbsp olive oil
100ml dry white wine
800g tomato *passata* or tomato pulp (*polpa di pomodoro*)
2 tbsp tomato pureé, diluted with 2 tbsp water
a few basil leaves, shredded

To make the beef olives, line up the escalopes side by side on your work surface. Make a stuffing mixture by combining the breadcrumbs, drained raisins, pine kernels, garlic, half the Parmesan and parsley, seasoning to taste. Divide the mixture evenly between the centres of the escalopes. Roll up each of the escalopes to enclose the stuffing and secure with a couple of wooden toothpicks.

Meanwhile, start to prepare the sauce by frying the onions in the olive oil in a large pan. When the onions are soft, after about 6–7 minutes, add the beef olives, and brown on each side. Add the wine and boil to allow the alcohol to evaporate. Add the tomato *passata* and the diluted tomato pureé and bring to the boil.

Reduce the heat, cover and let it bubble gently for 2 hours, turning the beef olives occasionally. When ready, add salt and pepper to taste and stir in the basil. Keep the beef olives separate from the sauce.

To make the pasta, pile the flour into a mound on a work surface and make a well in the middle. Add the egg and a splash of water. Gradually mix into the flour, adding enough water to bind the dough. Knead until smooth, then cover with a cloth and leave to rest for about 30 minutes.

Dust your work surface with a little flour and shape the dough a little at a time. Take a little piece of dough and roll it under the palm of your hand to make a baton, about 10cm long and 3mm in diameter. With a thin skewer, press the little baton around the skewer to make a spiral shape. Let the pasta spiral run down and off the skewer, then put on a cloth. Repeat to shape the rest of the dough.

Cook the pasta in plenty of boiling salted water until *al dente*, about 3–4 minutes. Drain and dress with the sauce.

Cut the beef olives into slices and arrange on top of the pasta. Scatter the remaining Parmesan over the pasta to serve.

Costolette di Agnello Ripiene

STUFFED LAMB CUTLETS

For this recipe the lamb cutlets have to be larger than usual, so that they can be stuffed. Get the butcher to cut eight cutlets on the bone, of 2.5–3cm thickness (which means a double cutlet, with the meat of two bones, one of the bones removed). These lamb cutlets are wonderful hot, but are also great cold as part of a picnic.

SERVES 4

8 large (double) young lamb cutlets,
  French trimmed, fat removed
2 slices Parma ham or *speck*, quartered
8 sage leaves
8 small pieces Fontina cheese, sliced
2 eggs, beaten with salt and pepper
about 6 tbsp dried white breadcrumbs (see page 33)
olive oil, for shallow-frying

With a sharp pointed knife, make an incision in the flesh of each cutlet, from the side opposite the bone, to make a pocket. Stuff the pockets with the ham, sage and cheese. Press the sides together to seal the cutlets. Dip the cutlets in the egg first, then coat well with breadcrumbs.

Pour enough olive oil into a large frying pan to cover the base generously and heat gently. Fry the cutlets until brown, about 5–6 minutes per side if you like them juicy as I do. Drain on kitchen paper and serve. *Zucchini e Fagiolini alla Menta* (see page 18) makes a delicious accompaniment.

Coniglio alla Cacciatora

HUNTER'S RABBIT STEW

When I was a boy, I was taught by my older brother how to kill (and skin) wild rabbits, and I remember the pride I felt taking such good meat home to my mother – and this was after the war when meat was hard to get. If you are unsure of how to cut the rabbit into pieces, ask your butcher to do it for you.

SERVES 4

1 x 1kg rabbit, cut into 8 pieces
plain flour, to dust
6 tbsp olive oil
2 garlic bulbs, skin on
1 small bunch rosemary
500ml dry white wine
400g ripe tomatoes, roughly chopped
salt and pepper
a little water or chicken stock, if necessary

Dust the pieces of rabbit with flour. Heat the oil in a casserole and brown the rabbit pieces on all sides. Add the garlic and rosemary and fry a little, then add the wine. Let the alcohol evaporate a little, and then add the tomatoes. Cover with the lid and let it come to the boil, stirring from time to time. Uncover and leave to stew slowly for 1 hour.

Add salt and pepper to taste, and a little water or stock if too dry.

The garlic will be soft, and particularly digestible because it has been cooked. Squeeze it in to your mouth and discard the tough skin. The stew can be eaten accompanied by polenta (see page 94) or bread.

LEFTOVERS
Make a sauce for pasta with any leftover meat and sauce. Take out the bones, chop the meat finely, add some fried onions and some torn basil. Check for seasoning, and add water or stock if too thick.

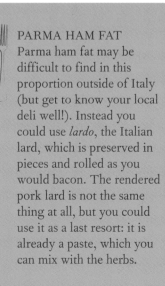

Anitra Arrosto con Grasso di Prosciutto

ROAST DUCK WITH PARMA HAM FAT

Where else would a dish like this be cooked if not in the 'fatherland' of poetry and pigs? Emilia Romagna, of course. The ducks of the area are the proper ones with large breasts and some natural fat, which are fed mainly on corn. The pigs are the famous animals which produce that wonderful fatty ham known here as Parma ham. This dish represents a perfect harmony between the two.

SERVES 4–6

200g Parma ham fat (from a friendly grocer),
   finely minced or chopped, or pork lard
10g black peppercorns, crushed
1 garlic clove, peeled and puréed
freshly grated nutmeg
a pinch of ground cinnamon
1 tbsp each of rosemary needles and sage leaves,
   finely chopped
1 x 2kg free-range duck
4 tbsp olive oil
salt

Preheat the oven to 200°C/Gas 6.

Mix the ham fat or lard with the peppercorns, garlic, a pinch of nutmeg, cinnamon, rosemary and sage until you have a solid paste.

In a roasting tin, coat the duck with the olive oil, and sprinkle a little salt inside and outside. Spread the fatty paste on to the duck breasts, then cover the roasting tin with foil. Roast the duck in the preheated oven for an hour. Remove the foil and return to the oven for a further 30 minutes, basting with the copious fat.

Serve the duck meat with pieces of the delicious skin.

Fegato di vitello con Cipolle

CALF'S LIVER WITH ONIONS

This dish is often found in Venice, where it is called *fegato all veneziano*. It can also be made with pork, lamb or chicken livers. Whichever you use, the result is always satisfying, and is particularly tasty when served with a purée of potatoes and celeriac.

SERVES 4

600g calf's liver, trimmed and finely sliced
plain flour, to dust
8 tbsp olive oil
600g white onions, peeled and very thinly sliced
50g raisins
20g caster sugar
4 tbsp white wine vinegar
salt and pepper

Dust the liver slices with flour.

Heat the olive oil in a large frying pan over a low heat (see page 22), add the onion and cook gently until soft, about 10–15 minutes.

Add the raisins, sugar and the flour-dusted liver and shallow-fry gently for 7 minutes, until cooked to your liking.

Pour in the vinegar and season with salt and pepper to taste, then stir to heat through. Serve immediately.

Trippa alla Fiorentina

FLORENTINE-STYLE VEAL TRIPE

Despite it being called *alla fiorentina* don't expect any spinach here! Tripe (the stomach of ruminants, usually cow) has become increasingly difficult to find, though Chinese food stores often stock a delicious type which is known in Italian as *millefoglie* ('thousand leaves' or 'leaf' or 'book' tripe in English). Failing that, try tender honeycomb tripe instead.

SERVES 4

1kg tripe (not bleached)
salt and pepper
8 tbsp olive oil
1 large onion, peeled and very finely chopped
2 carrots, peeled and cut into fine cubes
2 celery stalks with leaves, finely chopped
10 cherry tomatoes, halved
2 bay leaves
1 little sprig rosemary
150ml water or stock

Cut the tripe into small strips. Bring a large pan of salted water to the boil, add the tripe and cook for 5 minutes, then drain and set aside.

Heat the olive oil in a large pan, then add the onion, carrot, celery and tomatoes. Stir together and cook for 20 minutes, until the vegetables have softened.

Add the pre-boiled tripe, the bay leaves and rosemary, some salt and pepper to taste and the water or stock. Cover and cook for 2 hours or until the tripe is soft.

Spoon the tripe onto plates and serve accompanied with some bread.

Pesce
FISH

In all the regions around the coastlines of Italy, from the Gulf of Trieste to the Lagoon of Venice and then round towards the Marche, Abruzzi and Puglia, fish can be found on the daily menu in a multitude of recipes – often basically the same one, but with subtle changes from village to village. Italy also has many rivers and lakes which produce wonderful freshwater fish like tench, trout, carp and eel.

Eating fish is becoming more popular in Italy, but it is expensive because of dwindling stocks. There is a brilliant law in Italy whereby restaurants have to declare on the menu if the fish offered is fresh or frozen, the latter naturally being much cheaper.

Trota in Cartoccio

TROUT BAKED IN FOIL

This cooking method, designed to keep in all the juices and aromas, has been in use since Roman times. Then, they would cook foods enclosed in terracotta, while now we wrap in foil and oven-bake to achieve the same result. So long as the little packages are well sealed, you could also try cooking this on a charcoal grill.

SERVES 4

4 rainbow trout, about 250g each
32 thin slices of lemon
salt and pepper
1 little bunch chervil, divided into 4
1 bunch parsley, divided into 4
100g unsalted butter

Preheat the oven to 200°C/Gas 6. Have ready 4 pieces of foil large enough to wrap the fish fairly loosely.

Clean the trout and remove the scales and all the innards (or get your fishmonger to do this). Wash the trout, and dry them. Cut off the fins. Make 4 incisions in one side of each fish with a knife.

Arrange the 4 pieces of foil on your work surface, and on each, place 4 slices of lemon. In the cavity of each fish, put some salt and pepper, a quarter of the herbs and 15g butter, cut into small pieces. Close the trout and place each one on top of the lemon slices on the foil, cut-side up. Divide the remaining butter, in pieces, between the fish, rubbing into the cuts. Season each fish with salt and pepper, then add another 4 lemon slices to the top of each. Close the foil around each fish to produce a bag.

Bake in the preheated oven for just 20 minutes. The fish are delicious served with a simple boiled potato salad.

Sardine alla Griglia con Salmoriglio

GRILLED FRESH SARDINES WITH GREEN SALSA

These little fish, which, like mackerel, contain oils that are beneficial to our health, are popular throughout the Mediterranean. This quick, tasty dish can also be eaten in smaller portions as a wonderful *antipasto*.

SERVES 4

16 large fresh sardines, gutted and cleaned
salt and pepper
1 lemon, cut into quarters

SALMORIGLIO
150ml extra virgin olive oil
juice of 2 lemons, finely grated rind of 1
1 small chilli, finely chopped
1 garlic clove, peeled and very finely chopped
4 tbsp finely chopped parsley

Preheat the barbecue or charcoal grill to hot.

Mix the *salmoriglio* ingredients together in a small bowl.

Put the sardines directly onto a hot charcoal grill. Sprinkle them with salt, brush with a little of the *salmoriglio* and cook for 5 minutes per side. Serve the sardines either hot or cold, with the lemon quarters and the remainder of the *salmoriglio*.

Impepata di Molluschi

SHELLFISH FRICASSEE

Impepata is a southern Italian dialect word for a dish full of pepper, usuallly applied to a dish of black mussels, with a few other shellfish when available. I have suggested clams here, but some razor clams, if small enough, would be a delightful addition.

SERVES 4–6

100ml extra virgin olive oil
2 garlic cloves, peeled and coarsely chopped
1 small fresh red chilli, finely chopped
1.5kg black mussels, cleaned and prepared (see page 58)
1.5kg large clams, cleaned and prepared (see page 58)
500ml dry white wine
3 tbsp finely chopped flat-leaf parsley
abundant freshly and coarsely ground black pepper

Heat the olive oil in a large saucepan and fry the garlic and chilli for 1–2 minutes. Add all the shellfish, along with the wine and parsley. Put the lid on and cook until all the shells are open, about 4 minutes, shaking the pan occasionally. They should start to open quite quickly, but keep on the heat until all are open. Discard any shells that remain closed.

Add lots of black pepper. Stir well and serve in bowls, with lots of bread to mop up the sauce.

LEFTOVERS
Prepare a tomato sauce of either fresh or canned chopped tomatoes (see page 69) and add any leftover shellfish to make a delicious pasta sauce.

Insalata Di Mare

SEAFOOD SALAD

What could be more wonderful in the height of summer than a lovely, freshly made seafood salad, eaten with *grissini* and washed down with a glass or two of crisp, dry, chilled white wine! The combination of fish to choose from is endless. Here are some suggestions: small razor clams, clams, prawns, small octopus, squid, cuttlefish, black mussels, scallops, etc. The choice is yours.

SERVES 4

600g freshly prepared and raw seafood
  (see above)
salt and pepper
50ml extra virgin olive oil
juice of 1 lemon
2 garlic cloves, peeled and halved
2 tbsp finely chopped flat-leaf parsley

Cook the seafood for a few minutes in boiling salted water. Drain well and put in a large bowl.

Mix together the olive oil, lemon juice, garlic, parsley and lots of pepper, and dress the seafood. This salad can be eaten either hot or cold.

TIP
If you like garlic, but want the flavour to be gentler than above, then omit the two garlic cloves suggested, take a half clove instead, peel it and rub around the inside of the salad bowl you will use, before discarding.

Verdure
VEGETABLES

Vegetables in Italy are considered an important part of the diet. According to local environmental conditions, Italian farmers grow all sorts of interesting vegetables, which are almost always organically cultivated and sold in the area of production. This means fresh from field to table, which the Italians love.

Prepared today in the same way as they have been for centuries, Italian vegetable dishes are able to substitute for meat and fish without a hint of vegetarianism. For instance, I would much prefer to eat a wonderful *parmigiana di zucchini* than a boring piece of meat or fish. The following recipes can all be eaten by themselves as a main course, in smaller portions as an *antipasto*, or with meat and fish as a side dish.

Grigliata di vegetali

GRILLED VEGETABLES

Very fashionable, grilled vegetables are available in almost every restaurant, whether Italian or not. At home you could either charcoal-grill these on a barbecue or use a special cast-iron ridged grill pan. The most important thing to remember is to add flavour with a marinade into which you dip the vegetables and which you use for basting as well.

SERVES 4

1 aubergine, thinly sliced lengthways
2 courgettes, thinly sliced lengthways
1 red pepper, seeded and cut into strips
1 yellow pepper, seeded and cut into
  strips
4 tomatoes, halved

MARINADE
5 tbsp extra virgin olive oil
2 tbsp very finely chopped mint
2 tbsp very finely chopped basil
2 tbsp white wine vinegar
salt and pepper

Preheat a charcoal grill or ridged grill pan.

Prepare the marinade by mixing together all the ingredients. Dip the vegetables one by one into the marinade, place on the hot grill and cook

for a few minutes each side. You will have to do this in batches. Leave the cooking of the tomatoes until last as they will make the grill wet. When turning the vegetables on to the other side, baste with the rest of the marinade.

Eat either as accompaniment to main dishes, or as a first course.

Maccu con Radicchio

BROAD BEAN PURÉE WITH GRILLED RADICCHIO

Here I have purposely chosen two ingredients which hail from the two furthest apart regions of Italy, Sicily and the Veneto. *Maccu* (a Sicilian dialect word) is a purée of dried skinned broad beans, which is often eaten by itself or with some braised bitter vegetables like chicory or rape tops. Radicchio, grown in the Veneto, is a slightly bitter type of chicory, which compliments the *maccu* well.

SERVES 4

300g dried skinned broad beans, soaked overnight
extra virgin olive oil
1 garlic clove, peeled and sliced
4 heads radicchio or Belgian chicory, quartered
15g salted capers, soaked (see page 34)
50ml water
6 tbsp extra virgin olive oil
salt and pepper

Drain the broad beans, cover them with fresh water and cook slowly until dissolved into a purée, stirring from time to time, about 20 minutes. Heat 100ml of the olive oil with the garlic in a large pan until gently bubbling, not boiling. Put in the radicchio and capers and add the water. Put the lid on and braise until the radicchio is soft. After 15 minutes, take a sharp knife and pierce the base of the radicchio. If it goes in easily, the radicchio is ready.

Should the broad bean purée still not be very fine, put it through a food processor. Add 6 tbsp of extra virgin olive oil, and some salt and pepper. Serve the two on a plate next to one another and drizzle a little more extra virgin olive oil on top.

LEFTOVERS
If you are making a soup the next day, try adding some leftover *maccu* to it in order to thicken it and add extra flavour.

Caponata Siciliana

SICILIAN VEGETABLE STEW

Versatile, delicious and easy to make, *caponata* is probably Sicily's best-known dish. Throughout the centuries Sicily has been invaded and colonised by many other nations and many Sicilian recipes show influences from other cuisines. Here you will see that there are some hints of the French *ratatouille*, while the inclusion of raisins and pine kernels suggests some Arabic influences too.

SERVES 4–6

800g aubergine
1 large onion, peeled and chopped
2 tbsp olive oil
3 ripe tomatoes, cut into chunky cubes
1 tbsp tomato purée, diluted with a
   little water
1 tbsp caster sugar
1 tbsp salted capers, soaked (see page 34)

20 green pitted olives
1 tbsp white wine vinegar
chopped leaves and stalks of 1 head
   celery
1 tbsp raisins
salt and pepper
1 tbsp pine kernels (optional)

Cut the aubergine into 3cm chunks, soak in cold water for 5 minutes, then drain. This will stop the aubergine from absorbing too much oil.

Fry the onion in the olive oil in a large pan for a few minutes to soften. Put the aubergine chunks into the pan and fry until soft and tender, about 10 minutes. Add the tomatoes, diluted tomato purée, sugar, capers, olives, vinegar, celery leaves and stalks, raisins and some salt and pepper and stew slowly until everything is melted together, about 30 minutes.

Stir in the pine kernels, if desired, and serve either cold or warm as a side dish, or by itself with bread.

Torta di Spinaci e Carciofi

SPINACH AND ARTICHOKE TART

This is not dissimilar to the French *quiche* which, although most known for its Lorraine connections, is actually made all over France. In Liguria, a similar egg tart is made, the *torta pasqualina* (Easter tart), of which this vegetarian tart is a variant. It is delicious eaten either hot or cold.

SERVES 6

675g frozen shortcrust pastry
  (to cut corners)
olive oil
flour, to dust

FILLING
1kg spinach leaves, cleaned, washed
  and any tough stalks removed
salt and pepper

6 tbsp olive oil
2 onions, peeled and thinly sliced
100ml water
6 baby artichoke hearts, trimmed (see
  page 75) and sliced
300g fresh ricotta cheese
6 eggs, beaten
70g Parmesan, freshly grated
freshly grated nutmeg

Preheat the oven to 180°C/Gas 4. Use a little olive oil to grease a 25cm tart tin, then dust with a little flour.

Blanch the spinach in boiling salted water for about 3 minutes, then drain well. Using your hands, squeeze the spinach leaves to extract as much liquid as possible. Chop finely.

Heat the olive oil and fry the onions briefly in a large saucepan. Add the water and the artichokes, cover and cook until tender, about 20 minutes.

In a bowl, put the spinach, ricotta, beaten eggs, 50g of the Parmesan, a little nutmeg and some salt and pepper to taste. Mix together well.

Roll the pastry out until thin and use it to line the prepared tart tin. Pour the filling into the tin, sprinkle with the remaining Parmesan and bake in the preheated oven for 30 minutes. Leave to cool a little and serve.

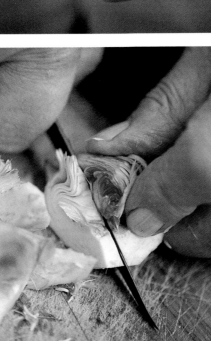

LEFTOVERS
If there is anything left over, you can eat it cold the next day with some bread. Because this dish is made with olive oil, it doesn't congeal, and the flavours will have benefitted from having some extra time to combine.

Parmigiana di zucchini

BAKED COURGETTES WITH TOMATO AND TALEGGIO

This is a variation on the well known *parmigiana melanzane*, the baked dish of aubergines with tomato and mozzarella. By using Taleggio instead of mozzarella and courgette in place of aubergine, I've made this dish a little lighter, but no less wonderful!

SERVES 6–8

olive oil, for shallow-frying
700g middle-sized courgettes, cut into
  5mm thick slices lengthways
400g Taleggio cheese, cubed
100g Parmesan, freshly grated
salt and pepper

TOMATO SAUCE
2 garlic cloves, peeled and finely sliced
6 tbsp olive oil
800g canned chopped tomatoes
10 basil leaves

BATTER
100g plain flour
4 eggs. beaten
freshly grated nutmeg

Preheat the oven to 200°C/Gas 6.

Make the tomato sauce by frying the garlic in the olive oil in a pan until soft, about 5 minutes. Add the tomatoes and basil, some salt and pepper to taste and cook gently for 20–30 minutes.

To make the batter, put the flour in a bowl, make a well in the centre and pour in the beaten eggs. Season with a little nutmeg and some salt and pepper, and mix well to a thickish batter.

In a frying pan, gently heat a little olive oil. Dip the courgette slices into the batter, and fry in batches in the hot oil until golden, about 3–4 minutes per side. Drain on kitchen paper and set aside.

Now to assemble the dish. Put a layer of courgette slices on the base of a baking dish. Pour over a little tomato sauce, and some of the cheeses and then get on with the next layer. Finish with the sauce and Parmesan.

Bake for 30 minutes in the preheated oven. Leave to cool before cutting into portions to serve.

Dolci

DESSERTS

Italians are not known for desserts based on cream (with the exception of ice-cream, of course!) often preferring to end a meal with ripe seasonal fruit.

The number and variety of fruit puddings in this chapter reflects this fact, as well as including a number of baked goods that are typical of Italy. The preparation of these usually revolves around special occasions like Christmas, Easter, birthdays and saints' days – as is the case with the *pastiera di grano*, an Easter cake/tart from Campania, based on whole wheat grains cooked with ricotta and candied peel. I offer a simpler ricotta tart here. Some of the pudding recipes here are very traditional, some are less so, and my mango with lime offering is very modern. Enjoy!

Pere al Vino Rosso

WILLIAMS PEARS IN RED WINE SAUCE

An autumnal recipe using ripe pears and an uncomplicated red wine. This simple dish is very Italian, and has loads of flavour.

SERVES 6

6 ripe Williams pears
400ml red wine
rind of 1 lemon, in pieces
150g caster sugar
whipped double cream (optional), to serve

Preheat the oven to 200°C/Gas 6.

Wash and put the pears upright in a suitably sized ovenproof container. You want them to fit snugly, without too much space between them.

Bake in the preheated oven for 30–40 minutes.

Remove the pears from the oven and pour over the wine. Sprinkle over the lemon rind and most of the sugar, reserving a small amount to spoon on top of the pears. Bake for another 20 minutes, by which time the wine will have reduced and thickened in consistency.

Put the pears in a glass bowl, cover with the red wine syrup and chill.

Divide between 6 plates and serve with the syrup and some whipped double cream, if desired.

Mango con Sciroppo di Limo

MANGO WITH LIME SYRUP

An extremely simple recipe with lots of fresh flavour. The best mango to use here would be the Alfonso variety from India, but this recipe will be a success whatever type you use.

SERVES 4

2 large ripe mangoes
4 small sprigs mint

LIME SYRUP
3 limes
100g caster sugar

To peel the mangoes, cut close to the large narrow stone along the length of the fruit on either side. You will have two rounded bits, and the stone. Cut the peel off the rounded bits and place the four pieces on a large plate.

To prepare the syrup, first cut the rind off the limes, leaving behind any pith. Slice this rind into thin strips. Squeeze the juice from the limes into a small pan and add the sugar. Simmer until the sugar has melted, then boil to reduce this liquid by half. Add the strips of rind and continue to simmer for a few minutes, until caramelised. Leave to cool.

Pour the cooled lime syrup over the mango halves and decorate with the mint sprigs.

Zabaione con Sugo di Cioccolato Amaro

ZABAGLIONE WITH BITTER CHOCOLATE SAUCE

This terrific dessert is easy to make, delicious warm or cold and can be used in many different ways. It can be either eaten as it is, accompanied by some polenta biscuits (see page 169), used as a filling for choux pastry buns, or made into a wonderful ice-cream.

SERVES 6

6 organic egg yolks
120g caster sugar
170ml Moscato Passito di Pantelleria,
  Marsala or Madeira

CHOCOLATE SAUCE
200g bitter chocolate, broken into
  pieces
100ml double cream

Put the egg yolks and sugar in a heatproof bowl (preferably a copper pan with a rounded base) and whisk for a few minutes to obtain a smooth and pure foam. Add the chosen dessert wine and mix well.

Have ready a pan of boiling water, in which the bowl will fit, without the base touching the water. Put the bowl in place in the pan, and beat continuously over the simmering water until the mixture starts to thicken.

Divide the mixture between 6 glasses and chill.

In the same way – in a bowl over a pan of hot water, base not touching the water – melt the chocolate carefully. Add the cream, and stir well until smooth.

Put this on the top of the zabaglione. You can eat this straightaway or chill it again before serving.

TO MAKE IT MORE SPECIAL
To turn the zabaglione into an ice-cream, fold in 250ml whipped double cream after cooking and cooling, place in an ice-cream maker and freeze. Alternatively, transfer to a shallow bowl and freeze for 1 hour until it begins to solidify. Whisk well with a fork, then return to the freezer. Repeat this process three more times, then freeze until firm.

Tiramisu

TIRAMISU

Tiramisu is now so internationally well known that it can be found absolutely everywhere. But this classic MOF MOF (Minimum of Fuss, Maximum of Flavour) recipe, which I created 30 years ago, is both simple and delicious. Try it, and you will discover that you instantly become a dessert maker!

MAKES 4 INDIVIDUAL TIRAMISUS

2 egg yolks
100g caster sugar
a few drops of good vanilla essence
400g mascarpone cheese
80ml single cream
a little milk, if needed
400ml strong espresso coffee
4 tbsp Kahlua or Tia Maria
18 Savoyard biscuits (or ladies' fingers, they
   need to be absorbent)
some bitter cocoa powder, to dust

In a small bowl, beat the egg yolks, 80g of the caster sugar and the vanilla essence together. In a second larger bowl, mix the mascarpone with the cream to make it thinner. Mix the mascarpone with the egg. Should the mixture be too dense, add a few drops of milk.

Mix the coffee, chosen liqueur and remaining caster sugar together in a third bowl. Dip the biscuits briefly into the coffee (don't let them absorb too much liquid) and use to line 4 individual ramekins, cutting them in half if necessary to fit. Put in a layer of the mascarpone mixture, then top with some more biscuits, finishing with mascarpone and filling the ramekins to the top. Dust the tops with a little cocoa powder and chill until ready to serve.

Torta di Ricotta

RICOTTA TART

Italians love ricotta – a by-product of the cheese-making process – and use it to produce both savoury and sweet dishes. The most important thing to remember about ricotta is that it must always be very fresh: if there is even the tiniest hint of sourness, the ricotta is off.

SERVES 6–8

50g butter
3–4 sheets of filo pastry (frozen)

FILLING
500g fresh ricotta cheese
120g caster sugar
5 eggs, separated
150g mix of orange and lemon rind,
  cut into small cubes
finely grated rind of 1 lemon
50g bitter chocolate, broken into small pieces

Preheat the oven to 180°C/Gas 4. Grease the inside of a 25cm flan tin with a little of the butter, melting the remainder in a pan over a low heat.

Line the tin with the filo pastry, brushing each sheet with some of the melted butter.

Put the ricotta in a bowl, and loosen the texture with a fork. Mix in 100g of the sugar and the egg yolks, followed by the cubes of rind, the grated rind and the chocolate. Mix well together.

In another bowl, beat the egg whites until stiff, then add the remaining sugar. Fold this carefully into the ricotta mixture using a large metal spoon, taking care not to lose the airiness of the whipped whites.

Spread this filling on to the filo pastry on the base of the tin. Brush melted butter over the remaining sheet or sheets of filo. With scissors, cut ribbons of buttered filo pastry and spread these decoratively on the tart.

Bake in the preheated oven for 30 minutes and leave to cool before serving.

Torta di Nocciole

HAZELNUT CAKE

The most intensive taste of hazelnuts comes from the *tonda gentile delle Langhe*, a hazelnut grown in the Langhe region of Piedmont. The hazelnut itself is full of flavour, but becomes even more special after a gentle toasting.

SERVES 8

100g unsalted butter
150g Piedmontese hazelnuts, shelled
125g caster sugar
4 large eggs, separated
30g plain flour

300g fresh ricotta cheese
1 tbsp finely grated lemon rind
200g apricot jam, slightly diluted with
  water
30g dark bitter chocolate, grated

Preheat the oven to 200°C/Gas 6. Use a little of the butter to grease a 25cm flan tin.

Toast the hazelnuts on a baking tray in the preheated oven until a golden colour, a few minutes only. Leave to cool and chop finely.

Soften the rest of the butter and beat together with 70g of the sugar in a large bowl. Add the egg yolks and beat until smooth, then add the flour and mix well.

In another bowl, stir the ricotta with a fork until smooth. Add the cooled chopped hazelnuts and the grated lemon rind.

Beat the egg whites separately in yet another bowl until stiff, then add the remaining sugar, beating until completely blended. Gently fold the yolk mixture into the white mixture with a large metal spoon until even, being careful to lose as little air from the whites as possible.

Spoon or pour the mixture into the prepared tin and bake in the preheated oven for 30 minutes. Take out and leave the cake to cool in the tin.

When cool, remove the cake from the tin, and place on a cake plate. Spread the jam on top and sprinkle over the grated chocolate to finish.

Biscotti di Polenta

POLENTA BISCUITS

I love polenta in every guise. In Piedmont where I spent my youth, there are many polenta biscuits, but none with the crispness I achieved by using *polenta svelta*, the quick polenta flour. These biscuits are wonderful as accompaniments to fresh fruit salads, or dipped into zabaglione.

MAKES ABOUT 50 BISCUITS

200g unsalted butter, softened
200g granulated sugar
300g quick polenta
100g plain flour
½ tsp baking powder
4 eggs, beaten
finely grated zest of 1 lemon

Preheat the oven to 200°C / Gas 6.

Mix all the ingredients together in a large bowl. Take a piping bag and fill it with the mixture. Pipe the mixture onto a greased baking tray in either little dots or S shapes. Leave a generous amount of space between the shapes as the biscuits will spread while cooking.

Bake in the preheated for 15 minutes, until golden.

Cool on a wire rack, and store in an airtight container.

Fruttini

FRUIT PASTELS

At Christmas I brought a box of *pâté de fruit* from France – the little cubes dusted with sugar tasted of real fruit, inspired me to create this recipe. These pastels can be made with either home-made or commercial jam and eaten either as *petits fours*, or with cheese for lunch.

MAKES 120 PASTELS

1kg jam of any kind
juice of 1 ½ lemons
a little vegetable oil
caster sugar, to dust

Put the jam and lemon juice in a pan and stir over a medium heat until the jam has softened and the mixture resembles a sticky paste.

Lightly grease a small ceramic try with the oil, pour in the mixture and leave to cool. Cut the mixture into small cubes and roll each into walnut-sized balls. Dust with sugar before placing into paper *petits fours* cases.

INDEX

Special thanks go to Alastair Hendy
for the breathtaking photography;
Anna Louise Naylor-Leyland and
Martha Wailes for the endless typing;
Susan Fleming for editing;
Rebecca Hetherston for recipe testing.
And to my agent Pat White, my
publisher Quadrille and those who
made the book possible: Alison Cathie,
Jane O'Shea, Claire Peters, Simon Davis
and Marina Asenjo.